Communications
in Computer and Information Science   **1104**

Commenced Publication in 2007
Founding and Former Series Editors:
Phoebe Chen, Alfredo Cuzzocrea, Xiaoyong Du, Orhun Kara, Ting Liu,
Krishna M. Sivalingam, Dominik Ślęzak, Takashi Washio, Xiaokang Yang,
and Junsong Yuan

More information about this series at http://www.springer.com/series/7899

Shujian Huang · Kevin Knight (Eds.)

Machine Translation

15th China Conference, CCMT 2019
Nanchang, China, September 27–29, 2019
Revised Selected Papers

Springer

Editors
Shujian Huang
Nanjing University
Nanjing, China

Kevin Knight
Didi Labs
University of Southern California
Marina Del Rey, CA, USA

ISSN 1865-0929   ISSN 1865-0937 (electronic)
Communications in Computer and Information Science
ISBN 978-981-15-1720-4   ISBN 978-981-15-1721-1 (eBook)
https://doi.org/10.1007/978-981-15-1721-1

This Springer imprint is published by the registered company Springer Nature Singapore Pte Ltd.
The registered company address is: 152 Beach Road, #21-01/04 Gateway East, Singapore 189721, Singapore

Preface

The China Conference on Machine Translation (CCMT), organized by the Chinese Information Processing Society of China (CIPSC), brings together researchers and practitioners in the area of machine translation, providing a forum for those in academia and industry to exchange and promote the latest development in methodologies, resources, projects, and products, with a special emphasis on the languages in China.

CCMT (previously known as CWMT) events have been successfully held in Xiamen (2005, 2011), Beijing (2006, 2008, 2010), Harbin (2007), Nanjing (2009), Xian (2012), Kunming (2013), Macau (2014), Hefei (2015), Urumqi (2016), Dalian (2017), and Wuyi (2018), featuring a variety of activities including an Open Source Systems Development (2006), two Strategic Meetings (2010, 2012), and eight Machine Translation Evaluations (2007, 2008, 2009, 2011, 2013, 2015, 2017, 2018). These activities have made a substantial impact on advancing the research and development of machine translation in China. The conference has been a highly productive forum for the progress of this area and considered a leading and important academic event in the natural language processing field in China.

This year, the 15th CCMT was held in Nanchang, China, at Jiangxi Normal University. This conference continued being the most important academic event dedicated to advancing machine translation research. It hosted the 9th Machine Translation Evaluation Campaign, featured two keynote speeches delivered by Lucia Specia (Imperial College London) and Tao Qin (Microsoft Research Asia), and two tutorials (CIPSC ATT 18) delivered by Jan Niehues (Maastricht University), Chenhui Chu (Osaka University), and Rui Wang (NICT). The conference also organized three panel discussions, bringing attention to the data augmentation techniques in machine translation, the applications of machine translation techniques, and the research and career development for Ph.D. students.

A total of 75 submissions (including 21 English papers and 54 Chinese papers) were received for the conference. All the papers were carefully reviewed in a double-blind manner and each paper was evaluated by at least three members of an International Scientific Committee. From the submissions, 10 English papers were accepted. These papers address all aspects of machine translation, including improvement of translation models and systems, translation quality estimation, bilingual lexicon induction, multi-model translation, etc. Apart from the scientific papers, the official report of the machine translation evaluation campaign is also included in the proceedings.

We would like to express our thanks to every person and institution involved in the organization of this conference, especially the members of the Program Committee, the machine translation evaluation campaign, the invited speakers, the local organization team, our generous sponsors, and the organizations that supported and promoted the event. Last but not least, we greatly appreciate Springer for publishing the proceedings.

September 2019

Shujian Huang

Organization

General Chair

Heyan Huang   Beijing Institute of Technology, China

Program Co-chairs

Shujian Huang   Nanjing University, China
Knight Kevin   DiDi Labs, USA

Evaluation Chair

Muyun Yang   Harbin Institute of Technology, China

Organizing Chair

Mingwen Wang   Jiangxi Normal University, China

Tutorial Co-chairs

Boxing Chen   Alibaba, China
Xiangyu Duan   Soochow University, China

Workshop Co-chairs

Shujie Liu   Microsoft Research Asia, China
Yang Feng   Institute of Computing Technology, Chinese Academy
    of Science, China

Publication Co-chairs

Hailong Cao   Harbin Institute of Technology, China
Yidong Chen   Xiamen University, China

Sponsorship Co-chairs

Chong Feng   Beijing Institute of Technology, China
Tong Xiao   Northeastern University, China

Publicity Co-chairs

Maoxi Li   Jiangxi Normal University, China
Cunli Mao   Kunming University of Science and Technology, China

Program Committee

Hailong Cao   Harbin Institute of Technology, China
Boxing Chen   Alibaba, China
Jiajun Chen   Nanjing University, China
Yidong Chen   Xiamen University, China
Yufeng Chen   Beijing Jiaotong University, China
Yong Cheng   Google, Inc., China
Jinhua Du   Dublin City University, Ireland
Xiangyu Duan   Soochow University, China
Chong Feng   Beijing Institute of Technology, China
Yanqing He   Institute of Scientific and Technical Information of China,
                           China
Zhongjun He   Baidu Inc., China
Guoping Huang   Tencent AI Lab, China
Shujian Huang   National Key Laboratory for Novel Software Technology,
                           Nanjing University, China
Wenbin Jiang   Baidu Inc., China
Yves Lepage   Waseda University, Japan
Junhui Li   Soochow University, China
Maoxi Li   Jiangxi Normal University, China
Lemao Liu   Tencent AI Lab, China
Qun Liu   Huawei Noah's Ark Lab, China
Shujie Liu   Microsoft Research Asia, Beijing, China
Yang Liu   Tsinghua University, China
Cunli Mao   Kunming University of Science and Technology, China
Haitao Mi   Ant Financial US, USA
Toshiaki Nakazawa   The University of Tokyo, Japan
Tao Qin   Microsoft Research Asia, China
Xing Shi   University of Southern California, USA
Linfeng Song   University of Rochester, USA
Jinsong Su   Xiamen University, China
Zhaopeng Tu   Tencent AI Lab, China
Masao Utiyama   NICT, Japan
Mingxuan Wang   ByteDance, China
Rui Wang   NICT, Japan
Shaonan Wang   National Laboratory of Pattern Recognition, Institute
                           of Automation, Chinese Academy of Sciences, China
Derek F. Wong   University of Macau, Macau, China
Hua Wu   Baidu Inc., China
Tong Xiao   Northeastern University, China

Deyi Xiong	Soochow University, China
Jinan Xu	Beijing Jiaotong University, China
Muyun Yang	Harbin Institute of Technology, China
Heng Yu	Alibaba, China
Dakun Zhang	SYSTRAN, France
Jiajun Zhang	Institute of Automation Chinese Academy of Sciences, China
Xiaojun Zhang	University of Stirling, UK
Tiejun Zhao	Harbin Institute of Technology, China
Renjie Zheng	Oregon State University, USA
Jingbo Zhu	Northeastern University, China

Organizer

Chinese Information Processing Society of China

Co-organizer

Jiangxi Normal University

Sponsors

Diamond Sponsor

Kingsoft AI

Platinum Sponsor

Global Tone Communication Technology Co., Ltd.

Gold Sponsors

Sogou Inc.

NiuTrans Research

Silver Sponsor

Tencent Technology Co., Ltd

Contents

Improving Bilingual Lexicon Induction
on Distant Language Pairs

Wenhao Zhu[1], Zhihao Zhou[1], Shujian Huang[1(✉)], Zhenya Lin[2],
Xiangsheng Zhou[2], Yaofeng Tu[2], and Jiajun Chen[1]

[1] Nanjing University, Nanjing 210023, China
{whzhu,zhouzh}@smail.nju.edu.cn,
{huangsj,chenjj}@nju.edu.cn
[2] ZTE Corporation, Shenzhen, China
{lin.zhenya,zhou.xiangsheng,tu.yaofeng}@zte.com.cn

Abstract. Aligning the representation spaces of two languages to induce a bilingual lexicon achieves attractive results on European language pairs. Unfortunately, current solutions perform terribly on distant language pairs. To address this problem, we analyze existing models for the lexicon induction task of distant language pairs, such as English-Chinese. We propose an framework for the task with improved preprocessing, mapping and inference accordingly. Experimental results show that our proposed approach enhances the accuracy of bilingual lexicons substantially on English-Chinese, as well as some other distant language pairs.

Keywords: Natural language processing · Machine translation · Bilingual lexicon induction

1 Introduction

The Lexical translation table (or bilingual lexicon) is an essential part of machine translation (MT). Traditionally, dictionaries for bilingual lexicons are composed manually, which involves massive expert knowledge and expense. Since the research showing that the representation spaces of two languages can be aligned through a simple linear mapping [9], bilingual lexicon induction (BLI) has achieved great success on English-Italy, English-German language pairs and is drawing increasingly attention recently [7,13,14].

However, existing BLI models perform much worse on distant language pairs [11]. Intuitively, larger distance between two languages does bring more difficulty in aligning the two representation spaces. But previous researches do not pay enough attention on why the accuracy of these methods degrades substantially on distant language pairs.

In this paper, we make deep analysis of typical BLI models, which consist of three steps: preprocessing, mapping and inference [1,3,12]. We discuss the obstacles for applying current model directly to distant language pairs, and try

© Springer Nature Singapore Pte Ltd. 2019
S. Huang and K. Knight (Eds.): CCMT 2019, CCIS 1104, pp. 1–10, 2019.
https://doi.org/10.1007/978-981-15-1721-1_1

to improve the induction performance on distant language pairs by improving each step correspondingly.

More specifically, in the preprocessing step, we verify that "center" [1] is the key operation which can bring great gain for performance; in mapping, we propose to use multiple local mappings instead of a single one; in inference, we propose an approximated searching algorithm to determine the hyper parameter K in the *CSLS* method [8], so that "topic words" could be successfully distinguished from "hub words".

To demonstrate effectiveness of our method, quantitative experiments are conducted on English-Chinese fasttext dataset [6]. Experimental results show that our methods could tackle observed weaknesses and the improved framework outperforms existing methods. Furthermore, we demonstrate that our approach can be applied to other distant language pairs as well.

2   Background

Given the word embedding of two languages as input, the task of bilingual lexicon induction is to align the two embedding spaces and retrieve word pairs (bilingual lexicons) as output for downstreaming tasks. There are two popular branches in researches of BLI. One is the supervised methods, which require aligned word pairs as a seed dictionary [1,3,12]. Another branch of research is unsupervised methods, such as self-learning [2,4] and GAN-based models [5,8,15]. Because unsupervised methods are extremely unstable on distant language pairs, we mainly discuss the supervised methods in this paper.

For convenience, we will use the following definitions throughout this paper. We denote source word embedding as $\hat{X} \in \mathbb{R}^{n \times d}$ and target word embedding as $\hat{Y} \in \mathbb{R}^{m \times d}$, each row of which represents a single word vector. We use $X \in \mathbb{R}^{t \times d}$ and $Y \in \mathbb{R}^{t \times d}$ to denote the word vectors of aligned word pairs. So the ith rows of X and Y represent words that are translation of each other.

Following Artetxe et al. [3], typical supervised BLI models consist of three main steps: preprocessing, mapping and inference, where the embedding of both languages are transformed; the mapping function is learned; and finally, the bilingual lexicon is inferred. We will briefly introduce these steps in the following subsections.

2.1   Preprocessing

In preprocessing, some simple operations are applied to transform the representation space before mapping. These operations aim at making embeddings in the two representation spaces distribute as similarly as possible. Taking source language embedding X as an example, Xing et al. [14] proposed the "unit" operation to ensure word vector X_{i*} is of unit length. Later, Artetxe et al. [1] proposed the "center" operation, which let the mean of each column vector X_{*i} to be 0. Besides, Artetxe et al. [3] presents several other operations, such as "whiten", "re-weight", "de-whiten", "reduction". Please refer to their original paper for details.

Previous research has demonstrated that all of them contribute to the improvement of model performance on close-related language pairs. However, there is no guidance on using these transformations for distant language pairs.

2.2 Mapping

After getting two transformed representation spaces, a mapping function could be learned to build the mapping between the two, so that the embedding vectors of aligned pairs stay as close as possible.

The function is usually a linear transformation matrix W. Mikolov et al. [9] treat it as a linear regression problem. The training objective function is to minimize the sum of squared Euclidean distances:

$$\arg\min_{W} \sum_i ||X_{i*}W - Y_{i*}||^2 \tag{1}$$

More generally, it can be rewritten into the matrix form of Frobenius norm:

$$\arg\min_{W} ||XW - Y||_F^2 \tag{2}$$

Xing et al. [14] propose to add an orthogonal constrain ($W^T W = I$) into the process, which keeps the monolingual invariance after mapping. The neural mapping with a hidden state [11] has also been tried but it suffers the severe overfitting problem. Up to now, orthogonal mapping has become a standard way to project language space.

With the mapping function, e.g. W, source embedding $\hat{X}$ and target embedding $\hat{Y}$ are expected to be projected into the same space.

2.3 Inference

For inference, retrieval methods are used to obtain translation pairs from the mapped space. For a given word x, its induction translation y is

$$\arg\min_{y} f(xW, y) \tag{3}$$

where f is the retrieval function.

Mikolov et al. [9] apply nearest neighbour (NN) to get the corresponding target word, where $\cos(\cdot, \cdot)$ is used as measure. Dinu et al. [7] find that NN approach will suffer severe "hubness problem". More specifically, hub is some meaningless target words which appear as the nearest neighbour of many source words. As a result, methods such as *invnn* [7], *invsoftmax* [12], and *CSLS* [8] are proposed to alleviate this problem.

Taking speed and accuracy into consideration, $CSLS$ is recognized as the best way to induce bilingual lexicons. It considers the mean similarity of a source word x to its target neighbour as:

$$r_T(xW) = \frac{1}{K} \sum_{y \in \mathcal{N}_T(xW)} \cos(xW, y) \tag{4}$$

where $\mathcal{N}_T(xW)$ is the K nearest target neighbours of source word x; K is a hyper-parameter, which is usually set as 10. $r_S(y)$ can be denoted in the same way. Thus the whole retrieval function of $CSLS$ is:

$$CSLS(xW, y) = 2\cos(xW, y) - r_T(xW) - r_S(y) \tag{5}$$

3 Improved Framework

Here we present our contributions to the three steps of the BLI tasks.

3.1 Preprocessing

Current preprocessing operations are weakly explainable. Simply stacking them can't ensure the same effect on distant language pairs. We provide an empirical analysis of the transformations with English-Chinese language pair as an example. We find that "unit" and "center" are the most important transformation, while other transformations do not bring significant improvement. Details of the empirical analysis are provided in the experiment section (Sect. 4.2).

3.2 Multiple Local Mappings

Previously all research papers use a single matrix W as transformation function based on the assumption that vector spaces have similar geometric arrangement [9]. However we doubt it's not held for distant language pairs and that's also the main reason why the model performance degrades under such settings. Experimental results show that a single mapping learns poorly on the training set, let alone the test set. Similar geometric distribution may only happens locally. A set of multiple local mappings $\{W_i\}_{i=1}^m$ rather a single mapping W better model BLI on distant pairs. The objective function of the local area centered at x_c is:

$$\arg \min_{W_i} \sum_{x_j \in \mathcal{N}_S(x_c)} ||x_j W_i - y_j||^2 \tag{6}$$

Following the objective and method described in Sect. 2.2, multiple local mappings $\{W_i\}_{i=1}^m$ can be obtained. Then given a source word x as a test case, the local mapping whose center is the closest to x will be applied to project it.

The remaining problem is how to produce multiple local mappings. In this paper, we propose to organize words by their topics. Assume topic word x_c are chosen as the center of a sub seed dictionary, such as "animals" or "politics", which summarizes a bunch of words. Analogous to $CSLS$, we define $\mathcal{N}_S(x_c)$ as K nearest source neighbour of x_c. For each word pair in the seed dictionary, word pairs surrounding x_c will be put into the sub seed dictionary $\{(x_i, y_i)$, where $x_i \in \mathcal{N}_S(x_c)\}$. In this way, multiple sub seed dictionaries centered at different topic words can be built for training multiple local mappings.

3.3 Approximated Searching

Though $CSLS$ enjoys success in its efficiency and low computation expense, it still faces some problems in practice. We find that $CSLS$ always confuses "topic words" with "hub words", as both have great similarity with neighbour words which always makes "topic words" punished wrongly as "hub words".

In Table 1. we list some wrong translation cases. For example, 液体 (liquid) is the so-called topic word. It is always mistaken as "hub words" by $CSLS$ so that it won't be chosen as candidate translation.

Table 1. Some representative wrong translation cases in which the $CSLS$ method punish "topic words" as "hub words" incorrectly.

Original Word	Translation Word	Ground Truth
液体 (liquid)	pressurizing	liquid
二手 (secondhand)	buyers	secondhand
反正 (anyway)	surprising	anyway

However, we find this phenomena can be changed by setting K value correctly. This is easy to explain when considering the difference between "topic words" and "hub words". When the parameter value is small, both topic word and hub words have great similarity with neighbour word which makes them hard to distinguish. As the value raises, it reaches the balance to translate both type of words correctly. Since the similarity between "topic words" and its neighbour word declines while it is not the case for "hub words". But if K gets too large, the accuracy will decline because hub words no more stay closed to its K-NN words.

In original paper, K is recommended to be set as 10. We observe that induction accuracy keeps raising if we increase K and then declines when K gets too large. Therefore we propose an approximated searching algorithm to choose K in $CSLS$ formula:

- increase K in step of 10 and compute model accuracy on the training set;
- once induction performance declines, we choose K in the last step as optimal value.

4   Experiments

4.1   Setup

All of the analysis are conducted on the fasttext dataset [6]. It provides word vectors of various languages in dimension 300 that are pretrained on Wikipedia corpus by skip-gram model [10] described in the paper of Bojanowski et al. [6]. The dataset also contains seed dictionary for different language pairs. According to source word frequency, the top 5000 words and their matched pairs make up for the training set. The top 5000 to 6500 words and their translation make up for the test set. The results are evaluated by the final accuracy of the retrieved bilingual lexicons on the test set.

We present detailed analysis about different steps (Sects. 4.2, 4.3 and 4.4) of the BLI models, with English-Chinese as an example language. Experiments of the whole improved framework are then presented, with a comparison to related studies, across multiple language pairs (Sect. 4.5). Further analysis are provided in Sect. 4.6.

4.2   Empirical Study of Transformations

We first compare the different transformations used in the preprocessing step. Following previous work [1], we take an orthogonal matrix as the mapping function and nearest neighbour as the retrieval method. The results are shown in Table 2.

Table 2. Accuracy of BLI models that take different combinations of preprocessing on English-Chinese.

unit	center	whiten	de-whiten	re-weight	reduction	Acc.
						27.33%
✓						27.13%
✓	✓					42.47%
✓	✓	✓				42.47%
✓	✓	✓	✓			42.47%
✓	✓	✓	✓	✓		42.47%
✓	✓	✓	✓	✓	✓	42.47%

The results show that "center" brings most performance gain and "unit" plus "center" is the optimal combination for distant language pairs. Additional transformation doesn't help enhancing accuracy but increases computational burden.

The possible explanation is that, for distant language pairs, two representation space are far from similar. "unit" and "center" are the simplest but effective way to normalize the two spaces, which enables the model to learn a high quality mapping more easily.

4.3   Employing Multiple Mapping Function

We then study the effect of mapping functions. We doubt whether a single mapping is suitable for distant language pairs since the results made by it is not satisfying. While two distributions differ significantly as a whole, but in the partial aspect the difference is smaller in our observation. Multiple mappings maybe a better solution, which project vector space part by part. We keep the setting of using "unit" and "center" in preprocessing and $CSLS$ as the retrieval method. We manually choose 10 topic words and divided the seed dictionary into 10 sub groups. Different local mappings are learnt for different groups.

Table 3. Train set accuracy (ACC_{tr}) and test set accuracy (ACC_{te}) of high quality local mappings on English-Chinese datasets. The last line is the accuracy of baseline. The next-to-last line is the average accuracy of representative groups.

topic word	train dict size	ACC_{tr}	test dict size	ACC_{te}
"animal"	1230	94.74	471	51.15
"culture"	1331	92.95	342	52.34
"education"	1315	92.60	351	51.24
Average		93.43		51.58
Single mapping		45.14		32.47

The results are listed in Table 3. For simplicity, we list the accuracy and related information of multiple mappings for three representative groups, with topic words "animal", "culture", "education", respectively. Both the representative groups and the average results show that the accuracy of using multiple local mappings is substantially better than a single global map for different groups. Besides, we find that the baseline model acts poorly on training set which indicates that a single mapping is far from perfect.

However, although multiple local mappings demonstrate their ability by considerable improvements, we do notice that automatically choosing the number of local mappings and selecting reasonable topic words for each mapping are difficult. At the current stage, this method is not integrated into our final system. We leave this as an important future work.

4.4   Inference with Approximated Searching

$CSLS$ usually fails to distinguish "topic words" from "hub words". But we find that it can be overcome by tuning K in the formula. To show the effect of different K, we take two language pairs (English-Chinese and English-German) as examples, and draw the accuracy curves as K changes in Fig. 1.

As we can see in Fig. 1, the curve keeps raising at the beginning and declines when K gets too large. To conclude, a medium K suits the case most. Our proposed approximated searching algorithm can quickly determine a medium K which ensure it achieves best performance in inference part.

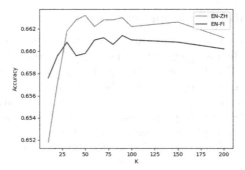

Fig. 1. Accuracy curve of the model when K in $CSLS$ formula changes. ("EN-ZH" is English-Chinese, "EN-FI" is English-Finnish)

Table 4. Precision for BLI task compared with previous work. The baseline model employs an orthogonal mapping as mapping function, $CSLS$ as retrieval metric and no preprocessing. ("EN" is English, "ZH" is Chinese, "JA" is Japanese, "KO" is Korean, "FI" is Finnish, "DE" is German)

| | Distant pairs | | | | Closed pairs |
	EN-ZH	EN-JA	EN-KO	EN-FI	EN-DE
Mikolov et al. [9,10]	13.27	14.16	16.11	32.47	61.20
Xing et al. [14]	27.13	2.54	24.64	38.67	68.13
Dinu et al. [7]	27.00	32.49	25.32	43.33	66.33
Artetxe et al. [1]	42.47	45.65	27.03	42.93	70.30
Smith et al. [12]	12.47	1.10	25.05	44.60	71.40
Nakashole et al. [11]	43.27	-	-	-	68.50
Baseline	32.47	1.71	31.47	47.60	73.37
uc + CSLS	45.33	51.68	31.54	65.76	79.02
Improved	**45.80**	**51.68**	**32.29**	**66.08**	**79.34**

4.5   The Improved Framework

Here we present the results of our final framework, which is a combination of following two improvements: the preprocessing with "unit" and "center" and $CSLS$ with our searching for K.

We conduct experiments on both distant and close language pairs and present results in Table 4. The last two line show performance gain brought by improved preprocessing and inference respectively. It's obvious that both parts contribute to the improvement of accuracy. On top of that, results show that the modified framework outperforms existing models on distant language pairs in particular. For distant language pairs, improved framework achieved more than ten percentage points on average above the baseline expect on English-Korean. For closed language pairs, the improvement is much smaller.

4.6   Further Analysis

Though improved lexicon quality has been achieved by our model, we still want to figure out what prevents the model inducing perfect lexicon. Therefore we contrast the error bilingual lexicons with the ground truth and find that the bad cases are mostly due to synonyms. Some representative mistakes are listed below in Table 5. We find that the BLI model is so smart that it predicts 舌头 (tongue) as ear's translation where they are already very closed. However the model is not smart enough to close the gap between 舌头 (tongue) and the true translation 耳朵 (ear).

Table 5. Some representative wrong translation pairs made by our improved framework on English-Chinese where predicted words have great similarity with correct translations.

Source Word	Predicted Word	Ground Truth
ear	舌头 (tongue)	耳朵 (ear)
myanmar	泰国 (thailand)	缅甸 (myanmar)
honey	柚子 (Pomelo)	蜂蜜 (honey)
plural	单数 (singular)	复数 (plural)

Therefore in future work, we want to close the gap and predict translation more precisely instead of choosing synonyms as the target translation. If this problem is alleviated, the performance of BLI model will boost.

5   Conclusion

In this paper, we make deep analysis on the English-Chinese word translation task where both languages are familiar to us. Based on comparison and analysis, we propose three methods to address observed problems. We present an improved framework with proposed methods for bilingual lexicon induction on distant language pairs. Experimental results demonstrate that our framework behaves excellently on distant language pairs and outperforms other existing models. Furthermore, we analyze wrong translations made by our framework and point out the gap that blocks model to perform perfectly on distant language pairs. In the future, we want to complete the algorithm of multiple local mappings and eliminate the effect brought by synonyms to predict translation more precisely.

Acknowledgement. We would like to thank the anonymous reviewers for their insightful comments. Shujian Huang is the corresponding author. This work is supported by the National Science Foundation of China (No. 61772261), the Jiangsu Provincial Research Foundation for Basic Research (No. BK20170074), "13th Five-Year" All-Army Common Information System Equipment Pre-Research Project (No. 31510040201). This work is also partially supported by the research funding from ZTE Corporation.

References

1. Artetxe, M., Labaka, G., Agirre, E.: Learning principled bilingual mappings of word embeddings while preserving monolingual invariance. In: Proceedings of Conference on Empirical Methods in Natural Language Processing, pp. 2289–2294 (2016)
2. Artetxe, M., Labaka, G., Agirre, E.: Learning bilingual word embeddings with (almost) no bilingual data. In: Proceedings of the 55th Annual Meeting of the Association for Computational Linguistics (Volume 1: Long Papers), pp. 451–462 (2017)
3. Artetxe, M., Labaka, G., Agirre, E.: Generalizing and improving bilingual word embedding mappings with a multi-step framework of linear transformations. In: AAAI Conference on Artificial Intelligence, pp. 5012–5019 (2018)
4. Artetxe, M., Labaka, G., Agirre, E.: A robust self-learning method for fully unsupervised cross-lingual mappings of word embeddings. In: Proceedings of the 56th Annual Meeting of the Association for Computational Linguistics, vol. 1, pp. 789–798 (2018)
5. Barone, A.: Towards cross-lingual distributed representations without parallel text trained with adversarial autoencoders. In: Meeting of the Association for Computational Linguistics, pp. 121–126 (2016)
6. Bojanowski, P., Grave, E., Joulin, A., Mikolov, T.: Enriching word vectors with subword information. Trans. Assoc. Comput. Linguist. 5(1), 135–146 (2017)
7. Dinu, G., Baroni, M.: Improving zero-shot learning by mitigating the hubness problem. In: International Conference on Learning Representations (2014)
8. Lample, G., Conneau, A., Ranzato, M., Denoyer, L., Jegou, H.: Word translation without parallel data. In: International Conference on Learning Representations (2018)
9. Mikolov, T., Le, Q.V., Sutskever, I.: Exploiting similarities among languages for machine translation (2013)
10. Mikolov, T., Sutskever, I., Chen, K., Corrado, G.S., Dean, J.: Distributed representations of words and phrases and their compositionality. In: Advances in Neural Information Processing Systems, pp. 3111–3119 (2013)
11. Nakashole, N.: NORMA: neighborhood sensitive maps for multilingual word embeddings. In: Proceedings of the 2018 Conference on Empirical Methods in Natural Language Processing, pp. 512–522. Association for Computational Linguistics, Brussels (2018)
12. Smith, S.L., Turban, D.H.P., Hamblin, S., Hammerla, N.Y.: Offline bilingual word vectors, orthogonal transformations and the inverted softmax. In: International Conference on Learning Representations (2017)
13. Vulic, I., Korhonen, A.: On the role of seed lexicons in learning bilingual word embeddings, vol. 1, pp. 247–257 (2016)
14. Xing, C., Wang, D., Liu, C., Lin, Y.: Normalized word embedding and orthogonal transform for bilingual word translation, pp. 1006–1011 (2015)
15. Zhang, M., Liu, Y., Luan, H., Sun, M.: Adversarial training for unsupervised bilingual lexicon induction, vol. 1, pp. 1959–1970 (2017)

Improving Quality Estimation of Machine Translation by Using Pre-trained Language Representation

Guoyi Miao[1], Hui Di[2], Jinan Xu[1($\boxtimes$)], Zhongcheng Yang[3],
Yufeng Chen[1], and Kazushige Ouchi[2]

[1] School of Computer and Information Technology, Beijing Jiaotong University,
Beijing, China
{gymiao,jaxu,chenyf}@bjtu.edu.cn
[2] Toshiba (China) Co., Ltd., Beijing, China
dihui@toshiba.com.cn, kazushige.ouchi@toshiba.co.jp
[3] Qihoo 360 Technology Co., Ltd., Beijing, China
yangzhongcheng@360.cn

Abstract. Translation quality estimation (QE) has been attracting increasing attention due to its potential to reduce post-editing human effort. However, QE still suffers heavily from the problem that the quality annotation data remain expensive and small. In this paper, we focus on overcoming the limitation of QE data and explore to utilize the high level latent features learned by the pre-trained language models to reduce the model's dependence on QE data and improve QE performance. Specifically, we propose two strategies to integrate the pre-trained language features into QE model: (1) a mixed integration model, where the pre-trained language features are fed into the QE mode combined with other features; and (2) a constrained integration model, where a constraint mechanism is used to adjust the reporting bias of our first integration model and enhance the robustness of the QE model. Experimental results on WMT17 QE task demonstrate the effectiveness of our approaches.

Keywords: Quality estimation · Machine translation · Pre-trained language model

1 Introduction

Neural Machine Translation (NMT) has become the state-of-the-art approach to machine translation in the recent years [1, 2]. However, the translation results of NMT are still not perfect, due to some big challenges such as the interpretability problem and the low-resource translation issue. To address this problem, human post-edits by applying insertion, deletion, and replacement operations are required on the translation outputs. Thus machine translation QE, which estimates the quality of translation output without reference at various granularity (sentence/word) levels, can play a crucial role for reducing human effort of post-editing.

Most studies treat QE as a supervised regression/classification task and train the QE model with quality-annotated parallel corpora, called QE data. Some of the previous

© Springer Nature Singapore Pte Ltd. 2019
S. Huang and K. Knight (Eds.): CCMT 2019, CCIS 1104, pp. 11–22, 2019.
https://doi.org/10.1007/978-981-15-1721-1_2

researches [3–5] employ useful QE features based on feature engineering work to improve QE. However, these manual features are usually expensively available. To solve this problem, some neural networks based models have been applied to QE task [6–9]. Among them, the recent bilingual expert model [9], which uses a bidirectional transformer [2] to construct their language model, achieves the state-of-the-art performance on most public available datasets of WMT17/WMT18 QE task.

Although the bilingual expert model performs well in extracting high level joint latent features, it still can't fully learn enough rich language features due to its single and solidified model architecture. On the other hand, recently some promising pre-trained language models have drawn much attention, such as ELMo [10], OpenAI GPT [11], BERT [12] and XLNet [22]. These models adopting diverse model architecture, first pretrain neural networks on large-scale unlabeled text corpora to learn rich language features, and then finetune the models on downstream tasks.

Inspired by these factors, we view the pre-trained language features as a useful supplement to low resource QE data and investigate the strategies of making full use of these features. Specifically, two strategies are proposed in this paper to integrate the pre-trained language representations into QE model:

(1) Mixed integration model: We use the recent bilingual expert model as our basic model and directly feed the pre-trained language features that are combined with the features learned by the bilingual expert model into the quality estimator of the QE model. That is, the pre-trained language representation is concatenated with the language representation of the bilingual expert model as input features for QE.

(2) Constrained integration model: We enhance the above integration model with a constraint mechanism by using bilingual alignment translation knowledge, which aims to adjust the reporting bias [21] of the pre-trained language features and improve the robustness of QE model.

The key contributions of this paper could be summarized as follows:

(1) We propose two simple yet effective strategies to integrate the pre-trained language features into QE models. Moreover, these strategies are of strong commonality and can be seamlessly applied to other QE models.

(2) We conduct extensive experiments on WMT17 sentence level and word level QE task and verify the effectiveness of the proposed method. Furthermore, we comprehensively analyze the effect of various types of pre-trained language models that are used in our models on QE task and conclude the reasons of these significant improvements.

2   Related Work

Our research is related to three topics, including NMT, pre-trained language representation, and QE for machine translation. We discuss these topics in the following.

2.1 Neural Machine Translation

Most Neural Machine Translation models are based on a sequence-to-sequence attentional framework [1, 2, 13–15], which contains an encoder and a decoder with an attention mechanism. Among them, transformer [2] is the dominant NMT model, which still follows the encoder-decoder architecture, but adopts self-attention networks to attend to the context and avoids recurrence completely to maximally parallelize training.

2.2 Pre-trained Language Model

Pre-trained language representations have shown the effectiveness to improve many natural language processing tasks [10–12, 16, 22]. Unlike traditional word type embeddings [17, 18], **ELMo** adopts left-to-right and right-to-left LSTM to train the word representations. Different from ELMo, **GPT** uses a left-to-right architecture, in which the previous tokens are considered in the self-attention layers of the transformer. Unlike GPT, **BERT** adopts a bidirectional transformer, which allows BERT to capture features from left and right context in all layers. Compared with previous models, **XLNet** is essentially order-aware with positional encodings, and it overcomes some limitations of BERT, such as the pretrain-finetune discrepancy.

2.3 Quality Estimation for Machine Translation

In recent years, there are many works using neural models to estimate the quality of machine translation. Kreutzer et al. [6] propose to use the representations of sentences obtained from neural network for word-level QE task. Kim et al. [8] introduce an entirely neural approach, which is based on a bidirectional and bilingual recurrent neural network (RNN) language model. Recently, Fan et al. [9] propose an end-to-end QE framework for automatically evaluating the quality of machine translation. In their model, a bidirectional transformer is used to build their novel conditional language model which is called neural bilingual expert model.

In this paper, we propose two strategies of integrating the pre-trained language features into our QE models, and our models are developed based on the bilingual expert model [9]. But, different from the bilingual expert model, our work focuses on exploring how to effectively use various pre-trained language models with different strategies to improve QE.

3 Method Description

In this section, we will describe our methods in details. We assume that the features learned by the pre-trained language models are highly related to the QE task and they can be viewed as an important supplement to the QE data. Under this assumption, we aim to explore the method of using the pre-trained language representations for QE task. In this research, we propose two strategies to integrate the pre-trained language representations into QE models and introduce two types of models: (1) mixed integration model, and (2) constrained integration model.

3.1   Mixed Integration Model

A pre-trained language model can learn rich and high level latent features on large unsupervised monolingual corpora, thus, a natural idea of exploiting the model comes out, that is, the features learned by the pre-trained language model can be fed into the QE model as input features. For our first method, we take advantage of the pre-trained language model in a simple and straightforward way. Specially, we follow the work [9] and construct our QE framework on the basis of the bilingual expert model. In our framework, we choose a pre-trained language model, such as ELMo, GPT, BERT and XLNet, as the feature extractor of our model respectively.

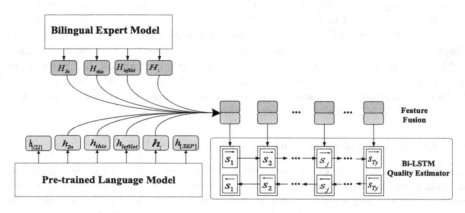

Fig. 1. Illustration of the mixed integration model.

Figure 1 illustrates our mixed integration model. The recent bilingual expert model is used as our baseline model and we directly feed the features learned by the pre-trained language models into the bilingual expert model. Then the feature vector from pre-trained language model is concatenated with the feature vector of the bilingual expert model as input for QE.

After that, the mixed features (from both the pre-trained language model and the bilingual expert language model) will be fed into a bidirectional LSTM quality estimator. For a sentence-level QE task, the hidden layer representation of the last time step is mapped to a real value within interval [0; 1] via a sigmoid function. For a word-level QE task, the hidden layer representation at each time step is mapped to a positive or negative category ('OK' or 'BAD' tag).

To handle the problem of out-of-vocabulary words, we use WordPiece [19] to segment the input words of the pre-trained language model, like BERT, and each word may be split into several sub-words. For example, the word ORENCIA is split into OR ##EN ##CI ##A, where "##" represents the separator symbol. Since the bilingual expert model does not conduct the segmentation, we add the vectors of several sub-words segmented from an original word, and the sum is used as the hidden layer representation of the original word.

3.2   Constrained Integration Model

Figure 2 illustrates our constrained integration model. The constrained integration model is a modification of the mixed integration model. That is, when predicting quality score, a constraint mechanism is added to adjust the final predicting score, which enhances the robustness of the QE model. Specifically, we extract and introduce bilingual alignment knowledge between source words and target words, which is similar to the information about faithfulness in translation, to adjust the bias of the features learned by the pre-trained language model. The word alignments table, called as A, are constructed by using the fast-align tool [20] with both source-to-target and target-to-source directions on bilingual parallel training datasets.

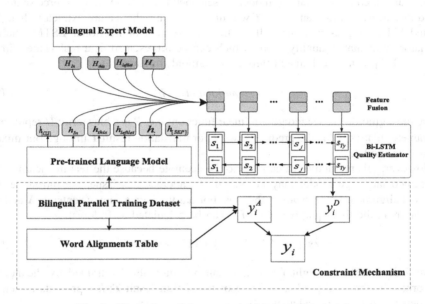

Fig. 2.   Illustration of the constrained integration model.

Definition. Given a source sentence $X = \{x_1, x_2, \cdots x_i, \cdots x_N\}$ and its corresponding translation sentence $T = \{t_1, t_2, \cdots t_j, \cdots t_K\}$, where $\langle X, T \rangle \in C$, C is the bilingual parallel training dataset, T contains K words and X contains N words. We call word a_i an **alignment word** of word t_j, if $\langle a_i, t_j \rangle \in A$ and $a_i \in X$. Assume all the words in sentence T have a total of N **alignment words**, where N can be statistically analyzed through the word alignments table, and assume that the number of co-occurrences of t_j and its **alignment word** a_i in the bilingual parallel training set C is M, t_j appears W times in C. Then we define both the sentence level alignment score and word level alignment score as y_i^A. The sentence level alignment score between X and T illustrates the alignment rate between source sentence and its target sentence in translation, and it can be represented as:

$$y_i^A = AlignS(X, T) = N/K \tag{1}$$

where we limit that $AlignS(X, T) \leq 1$.

The word level alignment score between word t_j and sentence X indicates their relevance, and it can be calculated by:

$$y_i^A = AlignW(t_j, X) = M/W \tag{2}$$

For our mixed integration QE model on sentence level QE task, the source sentence X and its corresponding translation T will first be fed into the feature extractor, then the learned hidden representations will be transferred to a bidirectional LSTM quality estimator, after that, a quality score, which can be represented as a real value within interval [0; 1], can be calculated through a sigmoid function:

$$y_i^D = sigmoid(h \cdot U + b) \tag{3}$$

where the sigmoid($\cdot$) is a standard nonlinear function; $b \in R$ is a bias term; U represents a parameter matrix; y_i^D is the predictive score for translation result T through our mixed integration model.

However, this predictive value may not be accurate because the features learned by pre-trained language model may be biased. To address this issue, we introduce the bilingual alignment score to adjust the bias. Formally, given a source sentence X and its translation T, the final quality score of T can be calculated as follows:

$$y_i = \lambda sigmoid(h \cdot U + b) + (1 - \lambda)AlignS(X, T) \tag{4}$$

where λ represents a weight factor that can be automatically trained by the neural network; y_i is the final predictive score of translation result T; h represents a weight parameter, and it can be calculated by:

$$h = \tanh(s \cdot W + b) \tag{5}$$

where s indicates the hidden state at the last time step of the LSTM network; W represents a parameter matrix.

The parameters in these above steps can be optimized through an end-to-end manner with the following object function:

$$loss = 1/n \sum_{i=1}^{n} \sqrt{(y_i - \hat{y}_i)^2} \tag{6}$$

where y_i is the predicted value of the translation result, and $\hat{y}_i$ is the true value.

Notation. For word level QE task, word t_j of the translation T will get a predictive value through Bi-LSTM quality estimator and sigmoid layer, and it will finally be mapped to a positive or negative category ('OK' or 'BAD' tag). The predictive score of word t_j can be formalized as:

$$y_i = \lambda sigmoid(h \cdot U + b) + (1 - \lambda)AlignW(t_j, X) \tag{7}$$

where h represents the hidden layer representation of word t_j.

4 Experiments

As we have presented above two different strategies to integrate the pre-trained language features into QE models, in the present section we report on a series of experiments on WMT17 QE tasks to test the effectiveness of the proposed strategies.

4.1 Datasets and Evaluation Metrics

We first train the bilingual expert model [9] with large-scale parallel corpus released for the WMT17/WMT18 News Machine Translation Task, which mainly consists of five data sets, including Europarl v7, Europarl v12, Europarl v13, Common Crawl corpus, and Rapid corpus of EU press releases. In addition, the data sets that we use for training the neural bilingual expert model also include parallel corpus released for the WMT17 QE Task, which contains source sentences and their corresponding post-edited translations. It can enable the bilingual expert model to learn more domain knowledge about the QE data. After data cleaning, the final training data contains about 6 M parallel sentence pairs. Then we test the proposed methods on German-to-English (de-en) and English-to-German (en-de) QE tasks. Specifically, we use 0.23 M sentence pairs for training, and 2 K sentence pairs for testing on de-en QE task. For en-de QE task, we use 0.25 M sentence pairs for training, and 2 K sentence pairs for testing.

For pre-trained language models, BERT uses Google's open source pre-trained version multi_cased Base[1]; ELMo uses the pre-trained Original (5.5B) version[2] of the open source framework AllenNLP; GPT uses open source pre-trained model[3] of OpenAI; and XLNet uses open pre-trained model[4] of Carnegie Mellon University.

In this paper we refer to the QE evaluation metrics of WMT. At sentence level, Pearson, MAE (Mean Absolute Error), RMSE (Root Mean Square Error), and Spearman are used as evaluation metrics. And at word level, we use F1-OK, F1-BAD, and F1-Multi to evaluate QE quality.

4.2 Baselines

To illustrate the effectiveness of our work, we compare our methods with the baseline method as follows:

---

[1] https://github.com/google-research/bert.

[2] https://allennlp.org/elmo.

[3] https://openai.com/blog/better-language-models.

[4] https://github.com/zihangdai/xlnet.

(1) Bi-Expert: this is the current strongest baseline QE model, called bilingual expert model, which adopts a language model based on a bidirectional transformer and achieves the state-of-the-art performance in most public available datasets of WMT 17/WMT18 QE task.

(2) Bi-Expert+ELMo: this is our mixed integration model, where ELMo is combined with the bilingual expert model as a feature extractor for QE.

(3) Bi-Expert+GPT: this is our mixed integration model, where GPT is combined with the bilingual expert model as a feature extractor for QE.

(4) Bi-Expert+BERT: this is our mixed integration model, where BERT is combined with the bilingual expert model as a feature extractor for QE.

(5) Bi-Expert+XLNet: this is our mixed integration model, where XLNet, the current state-of-the-art pre-trained language model, is combined with the bilingual expert model to produce features for QE.

(6) Bi-Expert+ELMo*: this is our constrained integration model, where a constraint mechanism is used to optimize the objective of integrating ELMo into QE model.

(7) Bi-Expert+GPT*: this is our constrained integration model, where a constraint mechanism is used to optimize the objective of integrating GPT into QE model.

(8) Bi-Expert+BERT*: this is our constrained integration model, where a constraint mechanism is used to optimize the objective of integrating BERT into QE model.

(9) Bi-Expert+XLNet*: this is our constrained integration model, where a constraint mechanism is used to optimize the objective of integrating XLNet into QE model.

It should be noted that, for each of the models described above, (2) to (5) are our mixed integration models, and (6) to (9) are our constrained integration models. The main difference between them is the way they are integrated and the pre-trained language features that are integrated.

4.3   Experimental Settings

The main training settings of bilingual expert model are set as the same as that in the work [9]. Specifically, the vocabulary size is set to 80000; the optimizer uses LazyAdam; the word vector size is set to 512; the block number is set to 2. Besides, the quality estimator adopts a bi-LSTM network, where dropout is set to 0.5, batch size is set to 64, and the hidden layer size is set to 128. To improve the quality of the parallel corpora, we filtered the source and target sentence with length ≤ 70 and the length ratio between 1/3 to 3. We applied byte-pair-encoding (BPE) [23] tokenization to reduce the number of unknown tokens on WMT18 News Machine Translation data sets.

4.4   Experimental Results

Tables 1 and 2 show the QE performance measured at sentence level and word level. It can be seen that, every one of the two QE methods we proposed, by using the pre-trained language features, improves the QE performance over all test sets in comparison to the baseline model-bilingual expert QE model.

Comparison with the Baseline Model. The experimental results in Table 1 indicate that each of the proposed models, whether our mixed integration model or our constrained integration model, can significantly improve the baseline model (bilingual expert model) on sentence level QE task, taking the evaluation metrics Pearson, MAE, RMSE, and Spearman into consideration. Specifically, our best mixed integration model Bi-Expert+XLNet can outperform the baseline model by 0.0154 points in term of Pearson's value, and our best constrained integration model Bi-Expert+XLNet* can improve the baseline model by 0.0206 points in term of Pearson's value on WMT17 de-en test data sets of sentence level QE task. Furthermore, at word level, the experimental results in Table 2 can also show the effectiveness of our two proposed methods on QE task. The above experimental results fully verify that the pre-trained language features are effective for the QE task.

Table 1. Comparison with the current strong baseline model (bilingual expert model, called as Bi-Expert) on **WMT17 de-en** test dataset of sentence level QE task. Row 2 to row 5 represent our mixed integration models, and row 6 to row 9 represent our constrained integration models.

# Models	Pearson's ↑	RMSE ↓	MAE ↓	Spearman ↑
1 Bi-Expert	0.6608	0.1577	0.1112	0.6355
2 Bi-Expert+ELMo	0.6643	0.1553	0.1110	0.6384
3 Bi-Expert+GPT	0.6661	0.1516	0.1092	0.6372
4 Bi-Expert+BERT	0.6747	0.1558	**0.0959**	0.6523
5 Bi-Expert+XLNet	**0.6762**	**0.1513**	0.0964	**0.6545**
6 Bi-Expert+ELMo*	0.6657	0.1542	0.1108	0.6376
7 Bi-Expert+GPT*	0.6695	0.1525	0.1041	0.6432
8 Bi-Expert+BERT*	0.6749	**0.1503**	0.0937	0.6539
9 Bi-Expert+XLNet*	**0.6814**	0.1524	**0.0923**	**0.6558**

Table 2. Comparison with the current strong baseline model (bilingual expert model, called as Bi-Expert) on **WMT17 de-en** test dataset of word level QE task.

# Models	F1-BAD	F1-OK	F1-Multi
1 Bi-Expert	0.4586	0.9363	0.4294
2 Bi-Expert+ELMo	0.5185	0.9438	0.4893
3 Bi-Expert+GPT	0.5179	0.9389	0.4888
4 Bi-Expert+BERT	0.5239	0.9405	0.4927
5 Bi-Expert+XLNet	**0.5286**	**0.9471**	**0.5006**
6 Bi-Expert+ELMo*	0.5194	0.9469	0.4918
7 Bi-Expert+GPT*	0.5166	0.9395	0.4853
8 Bi-Expert+BERT*	0.5270	0.9447	0.4979
9 Bi-Expert+XLNet*	**0.5352**	**0.9526**	**0.5098**

Comparison of our Two Proposed Methods. Experimental results in Tables 1 and 2 show that our proposed constrained integration method has better performance than the proposed mixed integration method for QE. Empirically, our best constrained integration model Bi-Expert+XLNet* can outperform the best mixed integration model

Bi-Expert+XLNet by about 0.0052 points in term of Pearson's value in Table 1. This phenomenon illustrates that our proposed constrained integration method can effectively optimize and denoise the pre-trained language features.

4.5   Analysis

The Effect of Pre-trained Language Models on QE Task. From the experimental results, we find out that XLNet and BERT improve the performance of QE more than other models do. We think it is due to the following three points: (1) The pre-trained language representations can contribute to the improvement of QE to some extent; (2) The ability of feature extraction of transformer is stronger than that of LSTM; (3) Bidirectional language model can capture more features than unidirectional language model can do.

Table 3. Results of sentence level QE on **WMT17 en-de** test dataset. Row 1 represents the current strong QE baseline model (bilingual expert model). Both row 2 and row 3 denote our proposed simple QE models that use BERT and XLNet as feature extractor respectively. Unlike our previous QE models, the pre-trained language features are the only source of features for QE in this model.

# Models	Pearson's ↑	RMSE ↓	MAE ↓	Spearman ↑
1 Bi-Expert	0.6842	**0.1453**	**0.1027**	0.7089
2 BERT+LSTM+MLP	0.6745	0.1539	0.1046	**0.7102**
3 XLNet+LSTM+MLP	**0.6857**	0.1486	0.1031	0.7054

Why Pre-trained Language Models Can Work? Experimental results on WMT17 sentence level and word level QE tasks show that the pre-trained high level latent language features learned by the pre-trained language model can contribute to the improvement of QE. However, this improvement is likely due to the use of a strong baseline system - bilingual expert model, since all of the proposed models are developed based on the bilingual expert model. To verify this assumption is not valid, we construct a simple additional QE model, which only consists of a pre-trained language mode, a LSTM and a Multilayer Perceptron (MLP) neural network, without using the bilingual expert model. The high-level joint features learned by a pre-trained language model are fed into a LSTM and a Multilayer Perceptron (MLP) neural network, and end up with a sigmoid function for estimating quality scores/categories. The experimental results on WMT17 en-de sentence level QE task are shown in Table 3. It is interesting that we find out the performance achieved by the two additional QE models (row 2 and row 3) is close to the performance achieved by the strong baseline model. We believe the reason for the improvement of QE is due to the strong feature learning ability of the pre-trained model itself. The pre-trained language model has learned a wealth of lexical, syntactic and semantic knowledge based on large corpus, so it can effectively alleviate the problem of feature sparseness of QE task.

5 Conclusion and Future Work

In this paper, we attempt to explore how to effectively improve QE with pre-trained language features learned by the pre-trained language models, and propose two strategies to integrate the pre-trained language features into QE models: (1) a mixed integration model, and (2) a constrained integration model. The first model uses a mixed method to treat the pre-trained language model as the feature extractor for QE model, and the second model is enhanced based on our first mixed integration model, which adjusts and optimizes the first model by using bilingual alignment knowledge. Experimental results on WMT17 QE task show that our proposed strategies can significantly improve the translation QE quality. In particular, our strategies are of strong commonality and can be seamlessly applied to other QE models.

In the future, we will explore how to apply transfer learning methods to QE task.

Acknowledgements. This work is supported by the National Nature Science Foundation of China (Nos. 61370130, 61976015, 61473294 and 61876198), the Fundamental Research Funds for the Central Universities (2015JBM033), the International Science and Technology Cooperation Program of China under grant No. K11F100010, the Fundamental Research Funds for the Central Universities (No. 2018YJS043), Major Projects of Fundamental Research on Philosophy and Social Sciences of Henan Education Department (2016-JCZD-022), and Toshiba (China) Co., Ltd.

References

1. Bahdanau, D., Cho, K., Bengio, Y.: Neural machine translation by jointly learning to align and translate. In: Proceedings of ICLR 2015 (2015)
2. Vaswani, A., et al.: Attention is all you need. arXiv preprint arXiv:1601.03317 (2017)
3. Felice, M., Specia, L.: Linguistic features for quality estimation. In: Proceedings of the 7th Workshop on Statistical Machine Translation, pp. 96–103. Association for Computational Linguistics (2012)
4. Specia, L., Shah, K., de Souza, J.G., Cohn, T.: QuEst - a translation quality estimation framework. In: Proceedings of the 51st Annual Meeting of the Association for Computational Linguistics: System Demonstrations, pp. 79–84. Association for Computational Linguistics (2013)
5. Kozlova, A., Shmatova, M., Frolov, A.: YSDA participation in the WMT 2016 quality estimation shared task. In: Proceedings of the 1st Conference on Machine Translation, pp. 793–799. Association for Computational Linguistics (2016)
6. Kreutzer, J., Schamoni, S., Riezler, S.: QUality estimation from ScraTCH (QUETCH): deep learning for word-level translation quality estimation. In: Proceedings of the 10th Workshop on Statistical Machine Translation, pp. 316–322. Association for Computational Linguistics (2015)
7. Martins, A.F.T., Astudillo, R., Hokamp, C., Kepler, F.: Unbabel's participation in the WMT16 wordlevel translation quality estimation shared task. In: Proceedings of the 1st Conference on Machine Translation, pp. 806–811. Association for Computational Linguistics (2016)

8. Kim, H., Jung, H.-Y., Kwon, H., Lee, J.-H., Na, S.-H.: Predictor-estimator: neural quality estimation based on target word prediction for machine translation. ACM Trans. Asian Low-Resour. Lang. Inf. Process. (TALLIP) 17(1), 3 (2017)
9. Fan, K., Wang, J., Li, B., et al.: "Bilingual Expert" can find translation errors. In: National Conference on Artificial Intelligence (2019)
10. Peters, M.E., Neumann, M., Iyyer, M., et al.: Deep contextualized word representations. arXiv preprint arXiv:1802.05365 (2018)
11. Radford, A., Narasimhan, K., Salimans, T., Sutskever, I.: Improving language understanding with unsupervised learning. Technical report, OpenAI (2018)
12. Devlin, J., Chang, M.W., Lee, K., et al.: Bert: pre-training of deep bidirectional transformers for language understanding. arXiv preprint arXiv:1810.04805 (2018)
13. Wu, Y., et al.: Google's neural machine translation system: Bridging the gap between human and machine translation. arXiv preprint arXiv:1609.08144 (2016)
14. Gehring, J., Auli, M., Grangier, D., Yarats, D., Dauphin, Y.N.: Convolutional sequence to sequence learning. arXiv preprint arXiv:1601.03317 (2017)
15. Luong, M.-T., Pham, H., Manning, C.D.: Effective approaches to attention-based neural machine translation. In: Proceedings of EMNLP 2015, pp. 1412–1421 (2015)
16. Dai, A.M., Le, Q.V.: Semi-supervised sequence learning. In: Advances in Neural Information Processing Systems, pp. 3079–3087 (2015)
17. Mikolov, T., Sutskever, I., Chen, K., Corrado, G.S., Dean, J.: Distributed representations of words and phrases and their compositionality. In: NIPS (2013)
18. Pennington, J., Socher, R., Manning, C.D.: Glove: global vectors for word representation. In: EMNLP (2014)
19. Wu, Y., Schuster, M., Chen, Z., et al.: Google's neural machine translation system: bridging the gap between human and machine translation. arXiv preprint arXiv:1609.08144 (2016)
20. Dyer, C., Chahuneau, V., Smith, N.A.: A simple, fast, and effective reparameterization of IBM model 2. In: Proceedings of NAACL 2013 (2013)
21. Gordon, J., Van Durme, B.: Reporting bias and knowledge acquisition. In: Proceedings of the 2013 Workshop on Automated Knowledge Base Construction, pp. 25–30. ACM (2013)
22. Yang, Z., Dai, Z., Yang, Y., et al.: XLNet: generalized autoregressive pretraining for language understanding. arXiv preprint arXiv:1906.08237 (2019)
23. Sennrich, R., Haddow, B., Birch, A.: Neural machine translation of rare words with subword units. In: Proceedings of ACL 2016, pp. 1715–1725 (2016)

Incorporating Syntactic Knowledge in Neural Quality Estimation for Machine Translation

Na Ye[✉], Yuanyuan Wang, and Dongfeng Cai

Human-Computer Intelligence Research Center,
Shenyang Aerospace University, Shenyang 110136, China
yena_1@126.com, yywang1005@qq.com, caidf@vip.163.com

Abstract. Translation quality estimation aims at evaluating the machine translation output without references. State-of-the-art quality estimation methods based on neural networks have certain capability of implicitly learning the syntactic information from sentence-aligned parallel corpus. However, they still fail to capture the deep structural syntactic details of the sentences. This paper proposes a method that explicitly incorporates source syntax in neural quality estimation. Specifically, the parse trees of source sentences are linearized, and the sequence labels are combined with the source sequence through hierarchical encoding to obtain a more complete and deeper source encoding vector. The hidden relationships between the source syntactic structure and the translation quality are modeled to discover the syntactic errors in the translation. Experimental results on WMT17 quality estimation datasets show that the sentence-level Pearson correlation score and the word-level F_1–mult score can both be improved by the syntactic knowledge.

Keywords: Quality estimation · Neural networks · Syntactic representation · Parse tree · Hierarchical encoding

1 Introduction

Recent years have seen great progress in the machine translation technology, especially with the rapid development of neural machine translation. However, the outputs of machine translation (MT) systems are still far from being error-free, and it is necessary to predict the post-editing effort needed for fixing the translations. One way to evaluate the machine translation results is comparing them with the reference translations as in the BLEU score. But the manually generated references are difficult to obtain in most cases. Therefore, the quality estimation (QE) technology aiming at estimating the quality of MT output without references attracted more and more interest.

The early studies of translation quality estimation are mostly based on feature engineering. The extracted features include baseline features such as n-grams, lengths and part-of-speech (POS), and translation quality features measuring fluency, adequacy and complexity [1]. To reduce the amount of features and the overlapping among them, feature selection methods such as Gaussian processes [2], heuristic methods [3] and partial least squares regression [4] are applied. Then machine learning models are trained to estimate the translation quality. Commonly used machine learning algorithms

© Springer Nature Singapore Pte Ltd. 2019
S. Huang and K. Knight (Eds.): CCMT 2019, CCIS 1104, pp. 23–34, 2019.
https://doi.org/10.1007/978-981-15-1721-1_3

include support vector regression [1], conditional random fields [4] and so on. The features employed by these methods are mostly shallow bilingual features.

With the development of deep learning technology in recent years, researchers began to extract deep features through neural networks [5–9]. Compared to traditional QE methods, neural quality estimation can discover deep bilingual semantic relationships and achieved advanced performance [10–13].

However, current neural QE methods treat a sentence as a sequence of words (or embeddings in the semantic space) and fail to capture the inherent syntactic structure of the sentence. In this paper we show that source syntax can be explicitly represented and incorporated in the neural QE framework to provide further improvements. We linearize the constituency tree or dependency tree of the source sentence, and combine the sequence labels with the source sequence through hierarchical encoding. In this way, the bilingual syntactic mappings are learned and the relationship between the source syntax and the target quality is built. The incorporation of syntactic knowledge can also alleviate the difficulty in estimating the translation quality of complex sentences. Experimental results on WMT17 QE datasets show that compared to current state of the art, the sentence-level Pearson correlation score increased by 1.92% and the word-level F_1–mult score increased by 2.12%.

2   Related Work

Some traditional QE methods attempted to apply syntactic features to the QE task. Hardmeier et al. [14] use tree kernel features extracted from bilingual parse trees to predict the post-editing costs of machine translated sentences. Experiments show that tree kernel features, whether used alone or in conjunction with other features, are beneficial to predicting post-editing costs. Rubino et al. [15] applied the syntactic features extracted from the output of different parsers to the QE task, which further proved the important role of syntactic features in QE. Specia et al. [16] combined the POS feature and the syntactic features based on dependency structure grammar and phrase structure grammar for QE task. Kaljah et al. [17] extracted 489 feature pairs from the constituency tree and dependency tree of the source and target languages. Finally 144 features are selected and combined with the baseline features and the tree kernel features for the QE task. Kozlova et al. [18] proposed numeric syntactic features including the width of bilingual parse tree, the depth of the tree, the proportion of internal nodes and the number of relative clauses and attributive clauses in the source language. Martins et al. [19] used syntactic features to detect the syntactic errors in machine translations in their LINEARQE sequence model. The adopted features include dependencies, head words, sibling nodes and parent nodes.

The above methods are based on traditional machine learning algorithms and have difficulty in combining the extracted syntactic features with deep semantic information, which makes the representation of syntactic features inadequate. The deep learning algorithms have strong capability of automatically learning feature representations, which can provide a flexible strategy for adding linguistic knowledge. Therefore, researchers tried to explicitly incorporate syntactic features into neural network models in many tasks. In the domain of neural machine translation, researchers incorporated syntactic information in the translation process [20–23] to solve the problem that RNN-based encoder-decoder architecture requires some supervision to effectively learn syntactic information [24–26]. In the domain of neural QE, Hokamp et al. [27] took advantage of the neural machine translation model to apply explicit features such as dependency labels and POS tags to word-level QE and achieved good performance. This method combines the post-editing task with the QE task and relies on the post-editing results to optimize the parameters in the process of model training. In our method, the post-editing results are not necessary, and we show the positive role of syntactic knowledge on both sentence-level and word-level QE and in different stages of QE. We also provided empirical analysis to better understand the contribution of syntax with different task granularities, different grammar types and different sentence lengths.

3   Syntactic Representation

Generally, syntactic structure can be represented or labelled by two types of grammar. One is the phrase structure grammar (PSG), and the other is the dependency structure grammar (DSG). In this paper we propose representation strategies for both types.

3.1   Representation for Phrase Structure Grammar

The phrase structure of a sentence includes all the constituents in the sentence and the hierarchical syntactic relationship among them. It can be expressed in the form of a constituency tree as shown in Fig. 1.

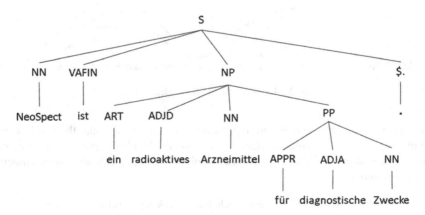

Fig. 1. Example of the constituency tree.

Li et al. [23] proposed mixed RNN encoding in neural machine translation. The constituency tree is linearly parsed into a sequence whose length is about 3 times that of the source sequence through depth-first traversal. In the QE task, in order to capture the intrinsic structure of the source sentence and build the relationship between each word and the constituents of its context while reducing the impact of sequence length on RNN, we linearize the constituency tree into phrase label sequences to represent the phrasal constituent of each word. Specifically, we take the parent node as the syntactic label for each leaf node. Table 1 gives an example of the representation for phrase structure grammar.

Table 1. Sequential syntactic labels for phrase structure grammar.

Source sentence	NeoSpect ist ein radioaktives Arzneimittel für diagnostische Zwecke
Constituency tree	((ROOT (S (NN NeoSpect) (VAFIN ist) (NP (ART ein) (ADJA radioaktives) (NN Arzneimittel) (PP (APPR für) (ADJA diagnostische) (NN Zwecke)))) ($..)))
Syntactic label	S S NP NP NP PP PP PP S

3.2 Representation for Dependency Structure Grammar

The dependency structure of a sentence implies the dependence relations between words to obtain local constituents of the sentence. The head contains the main grammatical and semantic information. The modifier is semantically subordinate to the head and plays the role of modifying and supplementing the head. Dependency structure can be expressed in the form of a dependency tree as shown in Fig. 2.

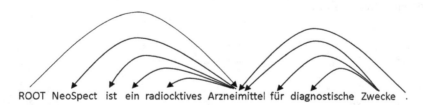

ROOT NeoSpect ist ein radiocktives Arzneimittel für diagnostische Zwecke .

Fig. 2. Example of the dependency tree.

Similar with the phrase structure representation strategy, we take the head of each word in a sentence as its syntactic label, and encode the label sequence in the same way as the source sequence. Table 2 gives an example of the representation for dependency structure grammar.

Table 2. Sequential syntactic labels for dependency structure grammar.

Source sentence	NeoSpect ist ein radioaktives Arzneimittel für diagnostische Zwecke
Dependency tree	[('ROOT', 0, 5), ('nsubj', 5, 1), ('cop', 5, 2), ('det', 5, 3), ('amod', 5, 4), ('case', 8, 6), ('amod', 8, 7), ('nmod', 5, 8), ('punct', 5, 9)]
Syntactic label	Arzneimittel Arzneimittel Arzneimittel Arzneimittel ROOT Zwecke Zwecke Arzneimittel Arzneimittel

4 Neural QE with Source Syntax

4.1 Model Architecture

Predictor-Estimator [7, 9] is one of the best-performing QE architectures available [10–13]. We also follow this architecture in our work. The neural networks comprise two sub-networks, namely predictor and estimator.

Predictor is a word prediction model which can be seemed as a feature extraction module. Given the source and the target sentences, a word in the target sentence is randomly selected and masked and recovered according to the source and target contexts. The model adopts the encoder-decoder framework [28] based on bi-directional RNN. The encoder encodes source sentence to a sentence vector c_j, and the decoder further reflects the context of the predicted target word. The predicted probability of the target word y_j is defined in terms of the source context x and the target context y_{-j} as follows:

$$p\left(y|y_1, \ldots, y_{j-1}, y_{j+1}, \ldots, y_{T_y}, x\right)$$
$$= g\left(\left[\vec{s}_{j-1}; \overleftarrow{s}_{j+1}\right], \left[y_{j-1}; y_{j+1}\right], c_j\right)$$

where g is a non-linear function which uses $\left[\vec{s}_{j-1}; \overleftarrow{s}_{j+1}\right]$, $\left[y_{j-1}; y_{j+1}\right]$ and c_j to predict the probability of the target word y_j. $\left[\vec{s}_{j-1}; \overleftarrow{s}_{j+1}\right]$ is the concatenation of $\vec{s}_{j-1}$ and $\overleftarrow{s}_{j+1}$. $\vec{s}_{j-1}$ and $\overleftarrow{s}_{j+1}$ refer to the hidden state of the forward RNN and the backward RNN in the target sentence. This value contains the quality information about whether the target word is correctly translated from the source sentence, so it is extracted in the form of quality vector as a bilingual feature.

Estimator takes the bilingual feature vectors extracted by the predictor module as input and builds a bidirectional RNN model. The probabilities of the word-level tags (OK/BAD) are calculated with the hidden states of each time step of the RNN, and the sentence-level HTER values (the percentage of editing required to correct the translation) are calculated with the output of the last step.

4.2 Syntax Modeling

We model the source sentence and its syntactic information with the multi-source approach [29].

The feature extraction module consists of two RNN encoders sharing parameters. One encoder maps the source sentence into a vector sequence $\left[\left[\vec{x}_1, \overleftarrow{x}_1\right], \left[\vec{x}_2, \overleftarrow{x}_2\right], \ldots, \left[\vec{x}_n, \overleftarrow{x}_n\right]\right]$. The other encodes the syntactic information of the source sentence and obtains a vector sequence $\left[\left[\vec{p}_1, \overleftarrow{p}_1\right], \left[\vec{p}_2, \overleftarrow{p}_2\right], \ldots, \left[\vec{p}_n, \overleftarrow{p}_n\right]\right]$. The two sequences are concatenated to form a vector sequence $\left[\left[\vec{x}_1, \vec{p}_1\right], \left[\vec{x}_2, \vec{p}_2\right], \ldots, \left[\vec{x}_n, \vec{p}_n\right]\right]$ which is more complete and sufficient in encoding the source language. This vector is taken as the final vector for decoding, enabling the quality vectors extracted in the decoding process to contain more syntactic knowledge.

In the QE module, two bi-directional LSTMs are used to build the model. In the sentence-level QE task, since the HTER value is a global score to measure the overall translation quality of the sentence, the prediction of HTER is treated as a regression problem. One of the bi-directional LSTM models is used to model the quality vectors, and the last hidden state of the forward and backward LSTM is concatenated as the final vector $\left[\vec{q}_m, \overleftarrow{q}_m\right]$. The other is used to encode the syntactic information of the source language, again using the last hidden state as the final vector $\left[\vec{p}_n, \overleftarrow{p}_n\right]$. The two vectors are concatenated and the HTER value is predicted with the sigmoid function. Word-level QE aims at predicting the accuracy of each word in the sentence, marking the correct words as OK and the wrong words as BAD. Therefore, it can be regarded as

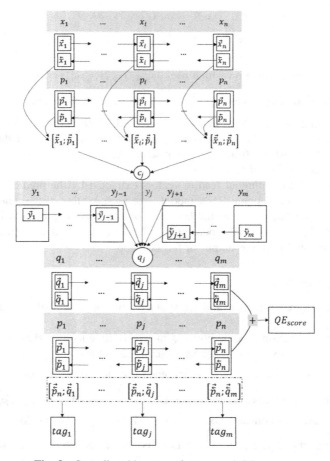

Fig. 3. Overall architecture of our neural QE system.

a binary classification or sequence labeling problem. Different from the sentence-level QE method, the last hidden state of the bidirectional LSTM $\left[\vec{p}_n, \overleftarrow{p}_n\right]$ that encodes the source syntax is concatenated with the hidden state of each time step of the bidirectional LSTM that models the quality vector. And this vector is used as the hidden state representation of the target word at each position.

The overall architecture of the neural QE system incorporating syntactic knowledge is shown in Fig. 3.

We applied the syntactic features of the source language to word-level and sentence-level tasks respectively. In order to test the effect of source language syntax on the QE module, we built two models with and without syntactic information in our experiments.

5 Experimentation

5.1 Experimental Settings

We evaluated the effectiveness of our method on German-English translation quality estimation task.

Two parts of corpora are used in our experiments. One is the large-scale bilingual dataset for training the feature extraction module. It comes from the parallel corpus of WMT machine translation task, including Europarl v7, Common Crawl corpus, News Commentary v11 and so on. In order to improve the performance of the experiment, we filtered the corpus and reserved the bilingual sentences less than 70 words and with bilingual word number ratio between 1/3 and 3. After filtering, about 4.5 million sentence pairs were obtained. The validation set contains 2489 pairs from Newstest2015. The other part of the corpora comes from WMT2017 QE task, which is used for training the QE module. The training set contains 25000 sentence pairs and the development set contains 1000 pairs. Since the labels of WMT2018 testing dataset has not been published, we choose the WMT2017 dataset for testing, which has 2000 sentence pairs in total.

We used the Berkeley Parser[1] to get the constituency trees of the source sentences, and the Stanford Parser[2] to get the dependency trees. The syntactic labels of the source language were extracted with the method described in Sect. 3. The statistics of the datasets are shown in Table 3.

Our QE systems are built upon the TensorFlow deep learning framework. Different network parameters are set for the feature extraction module and the QE module (see Table 4 for detail).

---

[1] https://github.com/slavpetrov/berkeleyparser.
[2] https://nlp.stanford.edu/software/lex-parser.shtml.

Table 3. Statistics of the bilingual dataset and the QE dataset.

Dataset	Data	Sentences
Bilingual dataset	Training	4,500,000
	Development	2489
QE dataset	Training	25,000
	Development	1,000
	Testing	2,000

Table 4. Neural network parameter settings.

Parameters	Predictor	Estimator
Layers	2	1
Hidden-dim	512	128
Word-dim	512	512
Batch size	64	64
Optimizer	Lazyadam	Lazyadam
Source vocabulary size	120000	120000
Target vocabulary size	120000	120000
Node type	LSTM	LSTM

5.2   Results and Analysis

We evaluated the proposed method on WMT17 testing set. For sentence-level QE, Pearson correlation score is used to measure the linear correlation between the predicted HTER value and the actual HTER value. For word-level QE, the performance is evaluated by F_1-mult, which is the product of F_1-OK and F_1-BAD.

Tables 5 and 6 give the experimental results of the sentence-level and the word-level QE task, respectively. We reimplemented the state-of-the-art system built on the predictor-estimator framework [7] as our baseline (referred to as P-E in the tables). P (+PSG)-E and P(+PSG)-E(+PSG) refer to the systems incorporating the PSG-based syntactic representations only in the predictor and in both predictor and estimator. Similarly, P(+DSG)-E and P(+DSG)-E(+DSG) refer to the systems incorporating the DSG-based syntactic representations.

Table 5. Results of the sentence-level QE task.

System	Pearson's r	Spearman's ρ	MAE	RMSE
P-E	0.6636	0.6013	0.1057	0.1452
P(+PSG)-E	0.6757	0.6117	0.1045	0.1431
P(+PSG)-E(+PSG)	0.6789	0.6133	0.1040	0.1425
P(+DSG)-E	0.6811	0.6146	0.1038	0.1422
P(+DSG)-E(+DSG)	**0.6828**	**0.6152**	**0.1034**	**0.1419**

Table 6. Results of the word-level QE task.

System	F_1-BAD	F_1-OK	F_1-mult
P-E	0.5486	0.9134	0.5011
P(+PSG)-E	0.5742	0.9042	0.5192
P(+PSG)-E(+PSG)	0.5713	0.9019	0.5153
P(+DSG)-E	0.5770	0.9052	**0.5223**
P(+DSG)-E(+DSG)	0.5720	0.9087	0.5198

From the above tables, we can see that both sentence-level and word-level QE are improved by adding syntactic knowledge. In the sentence-level task, the system with syntax modeling in both modules performs best, improving the Pearson correlation score by 1.92% compared to the baseline system. In the word-level task, the system with syntax modeling in only the predictor module performs best, improving the F_1-mult score by 2.12%.

According to the results, the systems with DSG perform better than those with PSG. This may be due to two reasons. First, phrase structure is more about the physical positional relationship between the constituents in the sentence. But dependency structure can reflect the deep semantic modification relationship between the words in a sentence, thus containing deeper syntactic information than phrase structure. Second, in our method, since the dependency labels are extracted from the source word sequence and combined with it, the two sequences are tied in a closer way. Therefore, coupling the source sequence with the DSG-based labels is more helpful to the feature extraction process.

Experimental results also show that for word-level QE, the performance of incorporating syntax in both predictor and estimator is not as good as in the predictor itself. We believe that this is because of the mismatching in the lengths of the syntactic sequence and the source sequence. We take only the last hidden state of the source syntax encoding as the syntactic representation for the whole sentence, and combine it with the quality vector of each word. This strategy is beneficial for the sentence-level regression problem, but it has some limitation in the word-level sequence labeling problem in affecting the quality vectors of the target words.

We also evaluated the effect of syntactic knowledge on complex sentences. It is difficult to directly measure the syntactic complexity of source sentences. However, the increase of sentence lengths is often accompanied by the increase of syntactic complexity. Therefore, we divided sentences into different lengths, and the sentences with similar lengths are classified into the same category, approximately indicating that the syntactic complexities of these sentences are similar. The experimental results of different sentence lengths on the sentence-level and word-level QE tasks are statistically analyzed as shown in Figs. 4 and 5.

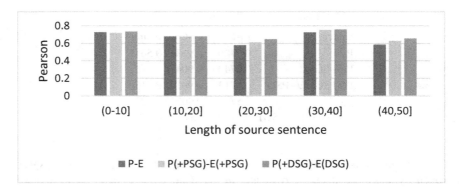

Fig. 4. Pearson correlation scores with respect to the lengths of the input sentences.

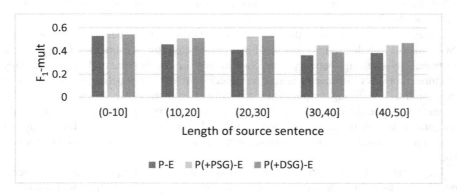

Fig. 5. F_1-mult scores with respect to the lengths of the input sentences.

In order to find out whether there is statistical difference between the systems which incorporate the syntactic representations and the baseline system, we made a significant difference analysis on the sentence-level QE task. The results showed that all the systems with syntax modeling significantly outperformed the baseline at the $p < 0.05$ level, especially the P(+PSG)-E(+PSG) and P(+DSG)-E systems significantly outperformed the baseline at the $p < 0.01$ level.

The figures show that when the sentence lengths are less than 20, the MT performance is good, and the bilingual syntactic structures tend to be consistent, so the effect of explicitly incorporating syntactic knowledge in the QE method is not obvious. However, with the increase of sentence lengths, the translation quality decreases, and the target syntactic structure tends to differ from the source structure. In these cases, our methods show their superiority, which proves that the syntactic information can effectively improve the QE accuracy of complex sentences by discovering the syntactic errors in the translation.

In terms of parameter amount and system speed, due to the large vocabulary used in the training process, the number of training parameters is relatively large. After introducing syntactic knowledge, about 10 million new parameters are introduced, and the training speed is slightly slower (about 10%) than the baseline system with a single GPU.

6   Conclusion and Future Work

This paper proposes a method that explicitly incorporates syntactic knowledge to address the inadequacy of syntactic feature extraction in the neural QE framework. Through extracting PSG-based and DSG-based syntactic labels and encoding them in the state-of-the-art predictor-estimator model, the syntactic information shows a positive impact on both sentence-level and word-level QE tasks.

In our method, in order to alleviate the long-distance dependency problem, only part of the phrase structure is used to guide the process of word prediction, which makes the PSG-based syntactic information insufficiently exploited. Therefore in the next step we will focus on further improving the syntax representation strategy. At the same time, the effect of syntactic knowledge is less prominent in the estimator module on word-level QE task. So we will also try to use an alignment mechanism to merge the syntactic labels and the quality vector sequence of the target words in our future work.

Acknowledgements. This work is supported by the Humanities and Social Sciences Foundation for the Youth Scholars of Ministry of Education of China (19YJC740107).

References

1. Specia, L., Shah, K., De Souza, J.G.C., et al.: QuEst-A translation quality estimation framework. In: Proceedings of ACL, pp. 79–84 (2013)
2. Shah, K., Cohn, T., Specia, L.: A bayesian non-linear method for feature selection in machine translation quality estimation. Mach. Transl. **29**(2), 101–125 (2015)
3. González-Rubio, J., Navarro-Cerdán, J.R., Casacuberta, F.: Dimensionality reduction methods for machine translation quality estimation. Mach. Transl. **27**(3–4), 281–301 (2013)
4. Han, A.L.F., Lu, Y., Wong, D.F., et al.: Quality estimation for machine translation using the joint method of evaluation criteria and statistical modeling. In: Proceedings of WMT, pp. 365–372 (2013)
5. Kreutzer, J., Schamoni, S., Riezler, S.: Quality estimation from ScraTCH(QUETCH): deep learning for word-level translation quality estimation. In: Proceedings of ACL, pp. 316–322 (2015)
6. Patel, R.N., Sasikumar, M.: Translation quality estimation using recurrent neural network. In: Proceedings of ACL, pp. 819–824 (2016)
7. Kim, H., Lee, J.H., Na, S.H.: Predictor-estimator using multilevel task learning with stack propagation for neural quality estimation. In: Proceedings of WMT, pp. 562–568 (2017)
8. Wang, J., Fan, K., Li, B., et al.: Alibaba submission for WMT18 quality estimation task. In: Proceedings of WMT, pp. 809–815 (2018)
9. Li, M., Xiang, Q., Chen, Z., et al.: A unified neural network for quality estimation of machine translation. IEICE Trans. Inf. Syst. **101**(9), 2417–2421 (2018)
10. Bojar, O., Chatterjee, R., Federmann, C., et al.: Findings of the 2015 workshop on statistical machine translation. In: Proceedings of WMT, pp. 1–46 (2015)

11. Bojar, O., Chatterjee, R., Federmann, C., et al.: Findings of the 2016 conference on machine translation. In: Proceedings of WMT, pp. 131–198 (2016)
12. Bojar, O., Chatterjee, R., Federmann, C., et al.: Findings of the 2017 conference on machine translation (WMT 2017). In: Proceedings of WMT, pp. 169–214 (2017)
13. Bojar, O., Chatterjee, R., Federmann, C., et al.: Findings of the 2018 conference on machine translation (WMT 2018). In: Proceedings of WMT, pp. 272–303 (2018)
14. Hardmeier, C., Nivre, J., Tiedemann, J.: Tree kernels for machine translation quality estimation. In: Proceedings of ACL, pp. 109–113 (2012)
15. Rubino, R., Foster, J., Wagner, J., et al.: DCU-Symantec submission for the WMT 2012 quality estimation task. In: Proceedings of ACL, pp. 138–144 (2012)
16. Specia, L., Giménez, J.: Combining confidence estimation and reference-based metrics for segment-level MT evaluation. In: Proceedings of AMTA (2010)
17. Kaljahi, R., Foster, J., Roturier, J., et al.: Quality estimation of English-French machine translation: a detailed study of the role of syntax. In: Proceedings of COLING, pp. 2052–2063 (2014)
18. Kozlova, A., Shmatova, M., Frolov, A.: YSDA participation in the WMT 2016 quality estimation shared task. In: Proceedings of WMT, pp. 793–799 (2016)
19. Martins, A.F.T., Junczys-Dowmunt, M., Kepler, F.N., et al.: Pushing the limits of translation quality estimation. TACL 5, 205–218 (2017)
20. Eriguchi, A., Hashimoto, K., Tsuruoka, Y.: Tree-to-sequence attentional neural machine translation. In: Proceedings of ACL, pp. 823–833 (2016)
21. Chen, H., Huang, S., Chiang, D., et al.: Improved neural machine translation with a syntax-aware encoder and decoder. In: Proceedings of ACL, pp. 1936–1947 (2017)
22. Currey, A., Heafield, K.: Multi-source syntactic neural machine translation. In: Proceedings of EMNLP, pp. 2961–2966 (2018)
23. Li, J., Xiong, D., Tu, Z., et al.: Modeling source syntax for neural machine translation. In: Proceedings of ACL, pp. 688–697 (2017)
24. Shi, X., Padhi, I., Knight, K.: Does string-based neural MT learn source syntax? In: Proceedings of EMNLP, pp. 1526–1534 (2016)
25. Linzen, T., Dupoux, E., Goldberg, Y.: Assessing the ability of LSTMs to learn syntax-sensitive dependencies. TACL 4, 521–535 (2016)
26. Graves, A.: Supervised Sequence Labelling with Recurrent Neural Networks. Studies in Computational Intelligence, vol. 385. Springer, Berlin (2008)
27. Hokamp, C.: Ensembling factored neural machine translation models for automatic post-editing and quality estimation. In: Proceedings of WMT, pp. 647–654 (2017)
28. Bahdanau, D., Cho, K., Bengio, Y.: Neural machine translation by jointly learning to align and translate. In: ICLR 2015 (2015)
29. Zoph, B., Knight, K.: Multi-source neural translation. In: Proceedings of NAACL, pp. 647–654 (2016)

Independent Fusion of Words and Image for Multimodal Machine Translation

Junteng Ma[1], Shihao Qin[1], Minping Chen[1], and Xia Li[1,2(✉)]

[1] School of Information Science and Technology,
Guangdong University of Foreign Studies, Guangzhou, China
juntengma@126.com, shihao_qin@126.com,
minpingchen@126.com, xiali@gdufs.edu.cn
[2] Guangzhou Key Laboratory of Multilingual Intelligent Processing,
Guangzhou, China

Abstract. Multimodal machine translation which combines visual information of image has become one of the research hotpots in recent years. Most of the existing works project the image feature into the text semantic space and merged into the model in different ways. Actually, different source words may capture different visual information. Therefore, we propose a multimodal neural machine translation (MNMT) model that integrates the words and visual information of image independently. The word itself and different key similarity information of an image are independently fused into the text semantics of the word, thereby assisting and enhancing the textual semantic and corresponding visual information of different words. And then we use them for the calculation of the context vector of the attention of decoder of our model. In this paper, different experiments are carried out on the original English-German sentence pairs of the multimodal machine translation dataset, Multi30k, and the Indonesian-Chinese sentence pairs which is manually annotated by human. Compared with the existing MNMT model based on RNN, our model has a better performance and proves the effectiveness of it.

Keywords: Multimodal machine translation · Image visual feature · Independent fusion · Attention mechanism

1 Introduction

Multimodal machine translation [1] is designed to create a machine translation model that can process information from multiple modalities, such as text, speech, video and image. Compared with the text-only neural machine translation (NMT) model, the multimodal neural machine translation (MNMT) model aims to achieve better translation performance by combining more information other then text. This paper is mainly for MNMT tasks that combine text and image.

Based on the advantages of MNMT models, multimodal neural machine translation studies have received a lot of attentions in recent years. Most of previous works use the image feature (including the global image feature and regional image feature) as a whole information to be fused into the model. For example, Vinyals et al. [2] used pretrained CNN as encoder of the seq2seq model, trying to capture different interaction

© Springer Nature Singapore Pte Ltd. 2019
S. Huang and K. Knight (Eds.): CCMT 2019, CCIS 1104, pp. 35–46, 2019.
https://doi.org/10.1007/978-981-15-1721-1_4

information of image and text in image caption task. Huang et al. [3] extracted the reginal features and the global features from image and regarded them as pseudo words as input to the end-to-end multimodal machine translation model. Calixto et al. [4] incorporated the global image features into the attention based NMT in three different ways so as to enhance the performance of the image on text-only machine translation.

These works integrate image features into the NMT model without considering that different words in a sentence may capture different semantic parts of an image. For example, the corresponding English source sentence of Fig. 1 is *"Three men in red and white striped shirts, white pants, and black hats hold flags."* In this sentence, we can see that the word *"shirts"* captures the visual semantic of the clothes in the image and the word *"striped"* captures the visual semantic of the design of the clothes in the image. If the image feature is simply fused into the model, like used as pseudo words, to initialize encoder or decoder's hidden state, the semantic information of different parts of an image and the words of source sentence cannot be obtained.

Fig. 1. A sample from dataset of multi30k. English: Three men in red and white striped shirts, white pants, and black hats hold flags. (Color figure online)

The work of Calixto et al. [5] and Caglayan et al. [6] take this into account, but they only consider them at the step of decoding time. Calixto et al. [5] proposed two separate attentions on the end of decoder to learn to attend to parts of the image and source words independently. Caglayan et al. [6] calculated a visual context vector at decoding time and concatenated them to the original context vector as one of their fusion models in MNMT. In fact, different words in the source sentence have different visual semantic information for different parts of the same image. And these independent semantic interaction information between source words and different parts of the same image can be used to enhance the context vector information at the end of decoder side, thus improving the overall translation performance. Therefore, each word itself can be independently fused with different key similarity semantic information of an image, these independent fusion information can be used to enhance the text semantics and visual information of each word of the sentence.

Based on this motivation, we propose a MNMT model that integrates the visual and text semantic information of words independently. The model use the extracted local image features, let their key visual information and each word semantic information in the source sentence independently fused into the word's new combined semantic space. It means that the combined semantic space of each source word contains the words semantic representation and the similarity of the word with different region semantics of the image. In this paper, we also propose to use max pooling on the local image features to extract global image representation to initialize decoder's hidden state. In this way, the decoder can consider the source words information as well as the different visual information corresponding to each word, and the whole information of the image, so as to better decoding and output of translated text. The main contributions of this paper are as follows:

(1) We propose a multimodal neural machine translation model that independently integrates the visual information and words' semantic information, so that encoder's output can capture different key features contained in an image and integrate them independently into the semantic space of the word itself. And we use it to calculate the attention of decoder, getting better context vector that contains text and visual information of different words. To the best of our knowledge, this is the first work that integrate different words and image independently as the end of encoder and use it for the attention on the end of decoder.

(2) We also apply max pooling on the extracted local image features to get global image feature. And we use it to initialize decoder's hidden state for further fusion of visual information. Experiments on Multi30k dataset shows that our model can improve the result on MNMT task.

2 Our Model

2.1 Architecture of Our Model

The framework of the classical Neural Machine Translation (NMT) is a sequence-to-sequence translation model based on encoder and decoder. The input end is the source language word sequence $X = (x_1, x_2, x_3, \ldots, x_M)$, and he output end is the target language word sequence $Y = (y_1, y_2, y_3, \ldots, y_N)$. The NMT model hopes to learn the maximum probability $P(Y \mid X)$ translated from X to Y, so as to learn the conditional probability distribution of training set data.

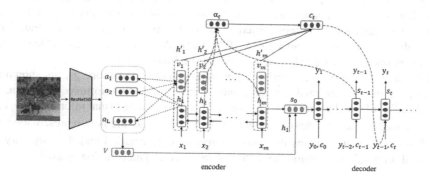

Fig. 2. The whole architecture of our model.

In this paper, we follow the work of Luong [9] which is the classical seq2seq NMT framework with attention mechanism, the architecture of our model is shown in Fig. 2. We will introduce our model from five parts: Encoder of our model, Independent fusion of words and image, Decoder of our model using visual semantic attention, Fusion of global visual features of image and Model training.

2.2 Encoder of Our Model

We use Bi-LSTM to encode the source language sentence. The forward LSTM receives the each word embedding and the previous LSTM cell's output from left to right and the output sequence is $\left(\overrightarrow{h_1}, \overrightarrow{h_2}, \ldots, \overrightarrow{h_N}\right)$. The backward LSTM receives the each word embedding and the previous LSTM cell's output from right to left and get $\left(\overleftarrow{h_1}, \overleftarrow{h_2}, \ldots, \overleftarrow{h_N}\right)$. Their calculations are shown in Eqs. (1) and (2). W_x is a source words embedding matrix. Each time step, the output hidden state is the concatenation of forward and backward's output $h_i = \left[\vec{h}_i; \overleftarrow{h}_i\right]$. So the final output of text words encoder is $h = (h_1, h_2, \ldots, h_N)$.

$$\vec{h}_i = f_{enc}\left(W_x[x_i], \vec{h}_{i-1}\right) \tag{1}$$

$$\overleftarrow{h}_i = f_{enc}\left(W_x[x_i], \overleftarrow{h}_{i+1}\right) \tag{2}$$

2.3 Independent Fusion of Words and Image

In order to get each word's corresponding visual information to the same image, we propose an independent fusion mechanism of words and image. Firstly, we calculate the similarity scores of each word and different local image features from the same image, and get the key visual information and concatenate it to the corresponding word's encoded hidden state.

The image features is extracted by the 50-layer Residual network (ResNet-50) of He et al. [7] which is pre-trained on ImageNet [8]. These local image features are activations of the res4f layer, which can be seen as encoding of image in a 14 * 14 regions, and each region is represented by a 1024 dimension features. We transform these 3 dimension features into a 196 * 1024 matrix $A = (a_1, a_2, \ldots, a_{196})$. Here a_j can be seen as one of the reginal visual feature of the image.

For each a_j, we use encoder's output h_i to calculate the score $g_{i,j}$, as shown in Eq. (3), we then normalized the score into probabilities using softmax operation, as shown in Eq. (4), and where L = 196. The h_i's corresponding visual information v_i can be calculated by Eq. (5). And we concatenate it to h_i to get the new representation h_i', which means that h_i' contains the words semantic representation and the similarity of the word with different region semantics of the image. The equation is as (6).

$$g_{i,j} = (h_i^T W_a)(W_{img} a_j) \tag{3}$$

$$\beta_{i,j} = \text{softmax}\left([g_{i,1}, g_{i,2}, .., g_{i,L}]\right)_j \tag{4}$$

$$v_i = \sum_{j=1}^{L} \beta_{i,j}(W_{img} a_j) \tag{5}$$

$$h_i' = [h_i^T W_a; v_i] \tag{6}$$

2.4 Decoder of Our Model Fusing Visual Semantic Attention

We use attention mechanism proposed by Luong et al. [9], so that the decoder can consider the current word's expected alignments information with the source words. The equations of attention mechanism are shown in (7)–(10).

Firstly, we compute an expected alignment $e_{t,i}$ between each source word's hidden state h_i, as in Eq. (7). We use h_i instead of h_i' in (6) which is concatenated with visual information is because that it will prevent the model from learning in our experiment. So here we still use h_i to compute the attention score. Then, we use softmax to normalize these expected alignments $e_{t,i}$ and get model's attention weights $\alpha_{t,i}$, shown as Eq. (8). And we use them and h_i' to compute the time-dependent context vector c_t, as shown in (9). So that the context vector c_t can contain both text and visual information at the same time.

Finally, the context vector c_t is used in computing the decoder's hidden state, as shown in Eq. (10), Where $W_y[\tilde{y}_{t-1}]$ is the word embedding predicted in previous time step, s_{t-1} is decoder's previous hidden state.

$$e_{t,i} = h_i^T W_a s_{t-1} \tag{7}$$

$$\alpha_{t,i} = \frac{exp(e_{t,i})}{\sum_{j=1}^{N} exp(e_{t,j})} \tag{8}$$

$$c_t = \sum_{i=1}^{N} \alpha_{t,i} h_i' \tag{9}$$

$$s_t = f_{dec}(W_y[\tilde{y}_{t-1}], s_{t-1}, c_t) \tag{10}$$

2.5 Fusion of Global Visual Features of Image

For better make use of the visual information, we propose to apply max pooling to get the global image feature, and use it to initialize decoder's hidden state. Firstly, we get the max value of each dimension for local image features. And input them to a feed forward neural network to project image features into the same vector space of decoder's hidden state. Together with the final output of encoder's two direction's LSTM to compute s_0, as shown in Eq. (11).

$$s_0 = \tanh\left(W_{di} \left[\vec{h}_N; \overleftarrow{h}_1 \right] + b_{di} + W_v V \right) \qquad (11)$$

2.6 Model Training

The model is trained and optimized by minimizing the negative loglikelihood, the equation are shown as (12) and (13), where θ is the parameter of the model, N is the number of samples in training set, x_n is the input sequence of source language, y_n is the output sequence of target language. And c_t is the context vector at decoding time step t, y_t is the target word and s_t is decoder's hidden state at time step t.

$$\min_{\theta} \frac{1}{N} \sum_{n=1}^{N} -log p_{\theta}(y_n | x_n) \qquad (12)$$

$$p(y_t | y_1, \ldots, y_{t-1}, x) = g(y_{t-1}, s_t, c_t) \qquad (13)$$

3 Experiment

3.1 Dataset

We use Multi30k[1] dataset as our dataset in the experiment. Multi30k dataset is a multilingual expansion of the original Flickr30k[2] dataset for image description generation task. Each image in Multi30k consists of an English sentence description and a German sentence translated by professional translators. In Multi30k, the training set, validation set and test set contains 29,000, 1,014 and 1,000 images respectively, each image has one sentence pair (the original English description and its German translation).

As for the preprocess of the dataset, we use Moses scripts[3] to tokenize, normalize-punctuation and trucase both English and German sentences. We use the training set of Multi30k to train the model, and validation set for model selection and test set for evaluation. We use BLEU4 [10] to measure the quality of the result.

3.2 Experiment Setup

We use Bi-LSTM as our encoder, both direction's hidden states are 512 dimensions. The source and target word embeddings are 512 dimensions and both are trained jointly with our model. Our decoder is a single direction LSTM with 512 dimensions hidden states. We choose Adam optimizer [11] with initial learning rate 0.001. The batch size is set to 40 and a total of 26 epochs are trained. If the perplexity of the model does not

---

[1] http://www.statmt.org/wmt16/multimodal-task.html.

[2] http://shannon.cs.illinois.edu/DenotationGraph/.

[3] https://github.com/moses-smt/mosesdecoder.

decrease on validation set for continuous 4 epochs, a learning rate decay mechanism is performed, decayed one-half of the original. We apply early stop when training the model, if the learning rate decay happens for 5 times, training is halted. Beam search [12] is used when translating on test and beam search size is 10.

3.3   Experimental Results and Analysis

In order to verify the performance of our model, we use several baseline models for comparison, they are Huang et al. [3], Calixto et al. [4], Calixto et al. [5], Caglayan et al. [6], and Elliott et al. [13].

The work of Huang et al. [3] proposed a MNMT model that fuses regional images, together with the entire image as pseudo words. The work of Calixto et al. [5] used two independent attention mechanisms for text and images, and their image features are extracted in the same way in the paper. The work of Calixto et al. [4] incorporated global image feature extracted by pre-trained VGG-19 [14] to initialize the decoder's hidden state. The work of Caglayan et al. [6] modulated each target embedding with global image feature, which is extracted by ResNet pool5 layer, using element-wise multiplication. The work of Elliott et al. [13] used the imagination method. They see multimodal translation into two sub-tasks, learning to translate and learning visually grounded representations.

Experimental Results on English to German

Table 1 shows the results on English to German sentence pairs of Multi30k. We carry experiments in 3 different methods to fuse image features. **Local_Only** only uses the regional image features that are independently fused with the source words encoded hidden states, **Global_Only** only use the transformed image features as the global representations to initialize the decoder's hidden state, and a combination of two methods is **Global_Local**.

As can be seen in Table 1, Local_Only performs better than the model of Calixto et al. [5] while using the same regional image features. For Calixto et al. [4] and Caglayan et al. [6] that only use global image representation, the result of our model of Local_Only improve 1.66 and 0.36 BLEU scores respectively. Moreover, our Global_Local model achieves best result in the experiments, which means that considering the overall information of the image and the key image visual features, the model can have different emphasis when translating, thereby improving the translation quality.

Table 1. The results on English to German sentence pairs.

	Models	BLEU4
Baseline	Huang et al. [3]	36.5
	Calixto et al. [4]	37.3
	Calixto et al. [5]	36.5
	Caglayan et al. [6]	37.8
	Elliott et al. [13]	36.8
Our method	Local_Only	38.16
	Global_Only	38.38
	Global + Local	**38.54**

Results on Indonesian to Chinese

In this paper, we also evaluate the model on low-resource language data. For this experiment, we manually translate the English and German sentence pairs of the validation and test set to Indonesian and Chinese. As for the training set of Multi30 k, we use Google translation[4] to translate the English to German sentence pairs into the corresponding Indonesian and Chinese.

Table 2 shows the results of our 3 different models and the baseline model is text-only NMT, which is based on attention mechanism and does not incorporate any visual information of the image. As we can see from Table 2, three MNMT models outperform the pure text-only NMT model. And Global_Local model still has best result and 1.92 BLEU scores higher than Text-Only NMT which shows that of the effectiveness of our model.

Table 2. The results on Indonesian to Chinese.

	Models	BLEU4
Baseline	Text-only NMT	27.48
Our method	Local_Only	28.80
	Global_Only	29.04
	Global + Local	**29.40**

3.4 Case Study

To better demonstrate the effectiveness our model, we conducted a case study of the results on the test set. Due to better understanding of the Chinese, we selecte the Indonesian to Chinese translation for case study. Figures 3 and 4 are the results of 2 cases from different models.

From Fig. 3, we can see the good translation quality of our model even on longer sentences. The Local_Global model translates more accurately and the phrases "白色卡车" and "白色建筑" are generated at the same time, while Local_Only and Global_Only only translate "白色卡车" and miss the latter. Local_Only and Local_Global accurately generates the "霓虹绿色安全背心" while Text_Only NMT does not translate the word "霓虹". When predicting the word "灰色", NMT does not do well while our multimodal models able to translate it successfully. It seems like that the MNMT can take into account the image features when translating.

Figure 4 shows that our three MNMT models accurately translate the colors of the characters in the images, while the Text_Only NMT still has a mistake. It prove again that the visual information helps enhance the translation quality. At the same time, Local_Only model miss the verb "穿着" which leads to the problem that the sentence is not smooth.

---

[4] https://translate.google.com/.

Source sentence:	Seorang pria yang mengenakan kemeja abu-abu, celana jeans biru dan rompi keselamatan hijau neon sedang berdiri di jalur kereta api dengan truk putih dan bangunan putih di latar belakang.
Reference:	穿着一件灰色衬衣，蓝色牛仔裤和霓虹绿色安全背心的一个人，站在铁路上，旁边是一辆白色卡车，背景是一栋白色的建筑。
Text-only NMT:	一个穿着<unk>衬衫，蓝色牛仔裤和绿色安全背心的男人站在铁轨上，背景是白色的卡车和白色建筑。
Local_Only:	一个穿着灰色衬衫，蓝色牛仔裤和霓虹绿色安全背心的男人站在铁轨上与白色卡车在背景中。
Global_Only:	穿着灰色衬衫，蓝色牛仔裤和绿色安全背心的男人站在铁轨上，背景中有白色卡车。
Local_Global:	一个穿着灰色衬衫，蓝色牛仔裤和霓虹绿色安全背心的男人站在铁轨上，背景是白色卡车和白色建筑。

Fig. 3. One case of translation comparision by different models.

Source sentence:	Tiga pria yang berkemeja bergaris-garis merah dan putih, celana putih, dan topi hitam memegang bendera.
Reference:	三名穿着红白色条纹衬衫，白色裤子和黑色帽子的男子举着旗帜。
Text-only NMT:	穿着红色和白色条纹衬衫，黑色裤子和黑色帽子的三名男子正举着旗帜。
Local_Only:	红色和白色条纹衬衫，白色裤子和黑色帽子的三名男子举着旗帜。
Global_Only:	穿着红色和白色条纹衬衫，白色裤子和黑色帽子的三名男子正拿着旗帜。
Local_Global:	穿着红色和白色条纹衬衫，白色裤子和黑色帽子的三名男子正拿着旗帜。

Fig. 4. Another case of translation comparision by different models. (Color figure online)

4 Related Work

Machine translation developed rapidly since statistical machine translation methods occurred [15–18], such as phrase-based statistical machine translation methods and other methods fused with different structures [19–21]. In recent years, machine translation has shifted from statistical-based methods to neural network based methods, and most of neural network based method focus on seq2seq model architecture.

In 2013, Kalchbrenner et al. [22] proposed a neural machine translation based on distributed continuous representation. This neural network apply an end-to-end method and it is an early research in the field of machine translation that propose the concept of NMT. Cho et al. [23] and Sutskever et al. [12] improved the mothod which better promoted machine translation based on neural network model. In subsequent studies, attention mechanism are used to NMTand achieve better results. Bahdanau et al. [24] introduced attention mechanism based on the work Cho et al. [23]. Luong et al. [9] improved on Bahdanau et al. [24] 's work and proposed local and global attention mechanism. Besides use RNN to implement seq2seq model, some researchers began to use CNN to build the model [25, 26]. Gehring et al. [27] proposed an encoder-decoder architecture totally based on CNN. Vaswani et al. [28] use Transformer for seq2seq modeling. Transformer abandoned the traditional RNN structure and only use self-attention for feature extraction, and achieved good result in text-only NMT.

Multimodal machine translation has become one of the research hotpots in recent years. Vinyals et al. [2] proposed a IDG model, which use pre-trained CNN as encoder of the seq2seq model. Calixto et al. [5] proposed two separate attentions on the end of decoder to learns to attend to parts of an image and source words independently. Huang et al. [3] used R-CNN [29] to obtain regional images, together with the entire image are input into VGG-19 to extract image features and regard them as pseudo words and input to the model. Calixto et al. [4] used the global image features and incorporated them in 3 ways: as pseudo words, to initialize encoder's and decoder's hidden state. Caglayan et al. [6] extracted global and local image features and try to fused them in different way.

Most existing RNN-based MNMT works have been done to fuse the visual information (global or local visual representation) of the image from different aspects to the model's encoder or decoder, to improve the performance of machine translation. However, since the key visual information of the image captured by each word is different, so we propose to capture independent key visual information for each word at encoding time step, and apply to attention mechanism. So the model can see the words' semantic information and the unique visual information of each word, so as to improve the translation result.

5   Conclusion

In this paper, we propose a multimodal machine translation model which integrates word and visual information independently for better decoding in the NMT model. By integrating each word itself with the different similarity information of the image into the text semantics of the word, the attention at the end of decoder can capture not only the word semantic but also the different parts of visual information, so as to have a better context vector of our model.

Our models were tested on the Multi30k dataset from English to German sentence pairs and from Indonesian to Chinese sentence pairs. The results show that the models we proposed have better improvement compared to the existing baseline system (integrate image visual semantic information into translation model by different aspects).

Especially in Indonesian-Chinese dataset which is a low-resource language dataset, the results of the experiments verify the validity of our proposed model in this paper.

In the future, we will further explore the multimodal machine translation from two aspects: (1) Further discuss the better extraction methods for different local and global features of images and improve the result of MNMT task; (2) Further discuss the research of MNMT model based on non-RNN, such as Transformer.

Acknowledgements. This work is supported by National Natural Science Foundation of China (61976062) and the Science and Technology Program of Guangzhou, China (201904010303).

References

1. Baltrusaitis, T., Ahuja, C., Morency, L.: Multimodal machine learning: a survey and taxonomy. In: IEEE Transactions on Pattern Analysis and Machine Intelligence, pp. 423–443 (2018)
2. Vinyals, O., Toshev, A., Bengio, S., Erhan, D.: Show and tell: a neural image caption generator. In: IEEE Conference on Computer Vision and Pattern Recognition (CVPR), pp. 3156–3164 (2014)
3. Huang, P.-Y., Liu, F., Shiang, S-R., Oh, J., Dyer, C.: Attention-based multimodal neural machine translation. In: Proceedings of the First Conference on Machine Translation, pp. 639–645 (2016)
4. Calixto, I., Liu, Q., Campbell, N.: Incorporating global visual features into attention-based neural machine translation. In: Proceedings of the 2017 Conference on Empirical Methods in Natural Language Processing (EMNLP), pp. 992–1003 (2017)
5. Calixto, I., Liu, Q., Campbell, N.: Doubly-Attentive decoder for multi-modal neural machine translation. In: Proceedings of the 55th Annual Meeting of the Association for Computational Linguistics, pp. 1913–1924 (2017)
6. Caglayan, O., Aransa, W., Bardet, A., Garcia-Martinez, M.,: Bougares, F., Barrault, L.: LIUM-CVC submissions for WMT 2017 multimodal translation task. In: Proceedings of the Conference on Machine Translation (WMT), pp. 432–439 (2017)
7. He, K., Zhang, X., Ren, S., Sun, J.: Deep residual learning for image recognition. In: 2016 IEEE Conference on Computer Vision and Pattern Recognition (CVPR) (2016)
8. Russakovsky, O., Deng, J., Su, H., et al.: ImageNet large scale visual recognition challenge. Int. J. Comput. Vis. **115**(3), 211–252 (2015)
9. Luong, M., Pham, H., Manning, C.: Effective approaches to attention-based neural machine translation. In: Proceedings of the 2015 Conference on Empirical Methods in Natural Language Processing (EMNLP), pp. 1412–1421 (2015)
10. Papineni, K., Roukos, S., Ward, T., Zhu, W.: BLEU: a method for automatic evaluation of machine translation. In: Proceedings of the 40th Annual Meeting of the Association for Computational Linguistics, pp. 311–318 (2002)
11. Kingma, D., Ba, J.: Adam: a method for stochastic optimization. In: International Conference on Learning Representations (ICLR) (2015)
12. Sutskever, I., Vinyals, O., Le, V.: Sequence to sequence learning with neural networks. In: Advances in Neural Information Processing Systems (2014)
13. Elliott, D., Kadar, A.: Imagination improves multimodal translation. In: Proceedings of the The 8th International Joint Conference on Natural Language Processing, pp. 130–141 (2017)

14. Simonyan, K., Zisserman, A.: Very deep convolutional networks for large-scale image recognition. In: International Conference on Learning Representations (ICLR), pp. 1–14 (2015)
15. Liu, Q.: Survey of statistical machine translation. J. Chin. Inf. Process. **17**(4), 2–13 (2003)
16. Brown, F., Cocke, J., Pietra, S., et al.: A statistical approach to machine translation. Comput. Linguist. **16**, 79–85 (1990)
17. Brown, F., Pietra, S., Pietra, V.: The mathematics of statistical machine translation: parameter estimation. Comput. Linguist. **19**(2), 263–311 (1993)
18. Och, F., Ney, H.: Discriminative training and maximum entropy models for statistical machine translation. In: Association for Computational Linguistics (2012)
19. Liu, Y., Wang, K., Zong, C., Su, K.: A unified framework and models for integrating translation memory into phrase-based statistical machine translation. Comput. Speech Lang. **54**, 176–206 (2019)
20. Zhang, J., Zong, C.: Learning a phrase-based translation model from monolingual data with application to domain adaptation. In: The 51st Annual Meeting of the Association for Computational Linguistics (ACL) (2013)
21. Tu, Z., Liu Y, Hwang, Y., Liu, Q., Lin, S.: Dependency forest for statistical machine translation. In: Proceedings of the 23rd International Conference on Computational Linguistics, pp. 1092–1100 (2010)
22. Kalchbrenner, N., Blunsom, P.: Recurrent continuous translation models. In: Proceedings of the 2013 Conference on Empirical Methods in Natural Language Processing (EMNLP), pp. 1700–1709 (2013)
23. Cho, K., Bahdanau, D., Bougares, F., Schwenk, H., Bengio, Y.: Learning phrase representations using RNN encoder-decoder for statistical machine translation. In: Proceedings of the 2014 Conference on Empirical Methods in Natural Language Processing (EMNLP), pp. 1724–1734 (2014)
24. Bahdanau, D., Cho, K., Bengio, Y.: Neural machine translation by jointly learning to align and translate. In: International Conference on Learning Representations (ICLR) (2015)
25. Bradbury, J., Merity, S., Xiong, C., Socher, R.: Quasi-recurrent neural networks. In: Association for the Advancement of Artificial Intelligence (2017)
26. Kalchbrenner, N., Espeholt, L., Karen, S., Oord, A., Graves, A., Kavukcuoglu, K.: Neural Machine Translation in Linear Time. arXiv preprint https://arxiv.org/abs/1610.10099 (2016)
27. Gehring, J., Auli, M., Grangier, D., Yarats, D, Dauphin, Y.: Convolutional sequence to sequence learning. In: Proceeding ICML 2017 Proceedings of the 34th International Conference on Machine Learning (2017)
28. Vaswani, A., Shazeer, N., Parmar, N., et al.: Attention Is All You Need. arXiv preprint https://arxiv.org/abs/1706.03762 (2017)
29. Ren, S., He, K., Girshick, R., Sun, J.: Faster R-CNN: towards real-time object detection with region proposal networks. In: Advances in Neural Information Processing Systems (NIPS) (2015)

Neural Machine Translation with Attention Based on a New Syntactic Branch Distance

Ru Peng[1], Zhitao Chen[1], Tianyong Hao[2($\boxtimes$)], and Yi Fang[1($\boxtimes$)]

[1] School of Information Engineering, Guangdong University of Technology,
Guangzhou, China
pengru709909347@gmail.com,
chenzhitao@mail2.gdut.edu.cn, fangyi@gdut.edu.cn
[2] School of Computer Science, South China Normal University,
Guangzhou, China
haoty@m.scnu.edu.cn

Abstract. Attention mechanism has been proved to be able to improve the quality of neural machine translation by selectively focusing on partial words of a source sentence during translation process. Attention mechanism usually focuses on local attention by using solely the linear index distance of words while ignores syntax structures of sentences. In this paper, we extend local attention through syntax distance constraint, and propose an attention mechanism based on a new syntactic branch distance, which simultaneously pays attention to words with similar linear index distances and syntax-related words. Based on the English-to-German translation task, experiment results showed that our model outperforms a recent baseline method with an improvement of 1.61 BLEU points, demonstrating the effectiveness of the proposed model.

Keywords: Neural machine translation · Attention mechanism · Syntactic branch distance · Syntax structure

1 Introduction

In the past few years, Neural Machine Translation (NMT) has made rapid progresses, showing superior performance compared to traditional statistical machine translation [1–3]. Many researchers have conducted extensive research on neural networks and attention mechanisms in NMT, which has promoted the rapid development of machine translation. Attention mechanism is critical to improve the translation performance of sentences in NMT. The research about attention mechanism has been in full swing. Bahdanau et al. [4] proposed an attentional NMT model (called global attention), which dynamically capture every contexts of source sentences in each decoding step, improving the performance of the NMT. Luong et al. [5] further refined global attention into local attention, selectively focusing source context of the fixed window size in each decoding step, and experimentally proved its effectiveness in German-to-English and English-to-German translation tasks. However, traditional attention mechanism, such as global attention [4] and local attention [5], only focuses on the sequential structure of sentences and ignores the dependencies between words. This does not

S. Huang and K. Knight (Eds.): CCMT 2019, CCIS 1104, pp. 47–57, 2019.
https://doi.org/10.1007/978-981-15-1721-1_5

conform to the rules of syntactic analysis, which may lead to some common syntax errors and affect the quality of the sentence translation.

In order to address the above problems, we propose a new attention mechanism based on the syntactic dependency tree of sentences. It simultaneously focuses on the sequential structure and syntactic structure of sentences for reducing the noise brought by grammar trees to some extent. In this paper, we propose a new syntactic branch distance constraint to extend local attention, predicting the encoder state associated with source words syntactically relating to target words. According to the dependency tree of a source sentence, a more effective context vector is calculated according to the syntactic branch distance for predicting target words. Experiments on the ISWLT2017 EN-DE translation task, our model is compared with a recent baseline method and the results show that our model improves 1.28 BLEU points over the baseline method.

2 Related Work

2.1 Syntax Representation for Neural Network

Researchers are devoted to integrating syntax information into the NMT system to improve translation performance. Eriguchi et al. [11] used tree LSTM, proposed by Kai et al. [6], to encode the HPSG syntax tree of the source sentence from bottom to top. Chen et al. [14] improved existed encoder with a tree encoder from top to bottom. Chen et al. [12] further extended through a bidirectional tree encoder to learn both sequence and tree structured source representations. Wang et al. [20] proposed a tree-based decoder, simultaneously generates a target-side tree topology and a translation, using the partially-generated tree to guide the translation process. Although these methods have achieved good results, the tree network used by the encoder and decoder makes training and decoding somehow slow and is not suitable for large-scale MT tasks.

There are other works that use syntax information, including grammar concepts, syntax tree structures and dependency units, and syntax trees for attention. Sennrich and Haddow [7] used part-of-speech tags, lemmatized forms and dependency labels to enhance the information carried by each word. In order to better integrate NMT with syntax trees, Eriguchi et al. [8] combined recursive neural network grammar with attention-based NMT system, encouraging models to combine grammatical prior knowledge for translation during training. Li et al. [9] linearized the constituent trees and encoded them with RNN. Wu et al. [10] proposed a sequence-to-dependency NMT model, using two RNNs to jointly generate target translations, and constructing their syntax dependency tree as context to improve word prediction. In order to better integrate NMT with dependency syntax trees, Wu et al. [13] further utilized the global knowledge from the source dependency tree to enrich each encoder state from child to head and head to child. Chen et al. [14] used local dependency unit to extend each source word to capture the long-distance dependency constraints of the source sentence and achieve a good translation of long sentences in NMT. Ahmed et al. [21] design a generalized attention framework for both dependency and constituency trees by encoding variants of decomposable attention inside a Tree-LSTM cell. These methods used grammar tags to extend source words and provide richer contextual information for word prediction. Due to the linear structure of the RNN, these methods were trained efficiently.

In this paper, we propose a new syntactic branch distance constraint to extend local attention and capture the encoder state associated with the source word syntactically relating to the target word. Rather than improving sequence encoder and decoder with a tree network direclty, we focus on the attention mechanism in the aspect of the syntactic branch distance of syntax tree without making any modifications to specific source representation on the basis of linearized representation using the Tree-LSTM coding syntax tree.

2.2   Attention Mechanism and Local Attention

Neural Machine Translation (NMT) commonly adopts the Encoder-Decoder [1] framework. NMT uses Recurrent Neural Network (RNN) architecture, such as Long Short-Term Memory (LSTM) or Gated Recurrent Unit (GRU) to obtain long-term dependencies. For a given word embedding sequence $X = x_1, x_2, \cdots, x_{|X|}$, encoder typically uses a bidirectional RNN to model the source word sequence and compute a hidden states representation h_i. That is, a forward encoder and a backward encoder encode sequence X to obtain the hidden sequences of the source sentence $H = h_1, h_2, \cdots, h_{|X|}$,

$$\vec{h}_i = f_1\left(\vec{h}_{i-1}, x_i\right) \tag{1}$$

$$\overleftarrow{h}_i = f_2\left(\overleftarrow{h}_{i-1}, x_i\right) \tag{2}$$

$$h_i = \left[\vec{h}_i, \overleftarrow{h}_i\right] \tag{3}$$

where f_1 and f_2 are either GRU($\bullet$) or LSTM ($\bullet$).

The decoder generally adopts conditional RNN with attention mechanism, and predicts the target sentence $Y = y_1, y_2, \cdots, y_{|Y|}$ literally according to the conditional probability $P(y_i)$. The prediction of word in current time step is calculated by the hidden state vector s_t, the last generated word y_{t-1}, and the context vector c_t, using Eq. (5) and (6), where g is a nonlinear function ans f_3 are either GRU($\bullet$) or LSTM ($\bullet$).

And the loss function of NMT model is defined as Eq. (4):

$$loss_{word} = \sum\nolimits_{t=1}^{Y} - \log p(y_t|y_{<t}; x) \tag{4}$$

$$p(y_t|y_{<t}; x) = g(y_{t-1}, s_t, c_t) \tag{5}$$

$$S_t = f_3(s_{t-1}, y_{t-1}, C_t) \tag{6}$$

The context vector c_t depends on a sequence of source annotations $H = h_1, h_2, \cdots, h_{|X|}$. Each annotation h_i contains information about the whole source word sequence with a strong focus on the parts surrounding the *i-th* word of the source word sequence. Here we explain below how the context vector c_t are computed in local attention in detail.

Compared with global attention focusing on all context information, local attention selectively focuses on a small context window, which can effectively reduce the computational cost. At the decoding time step i, alignment position p_i is generated for each target word of the batch of sentences using Eq. (7),

$$p_i = S \cdot \text{sigmoid}\left(v^T \tanh(W_p h_i)\right), \ p_i \in [0, S] \tag{7}$$

where S is the length of the source sentence, h_i is the decoder hidden state, and v^T and W_p are model parameters. The context vector c_t is then calculated as the weighted sum of the encoder states within the window $[p_i - D, \ p_i + D]$, where D is the empirical value typically set to 10. Therefore, the weight a_{ij}^l of each source annotation h_i is as follows.

$$\alpha_{ij}^l = \begin{cases} \alpha_{ij} \exp\left(-\frac{(s-p_i)^2}{2\sigma^2}\right), & s \in [p_i - D, p_i + D] \\ 0, & s \notin [p_i - D, p_i + D] \end{cases} \tag{8}$$

The standard deviation σ of the Gaussian distribution is empirically set to $D/2$. In addition, local attention is paid to the source annotations in the window $[p_i - D, p_i + D]$ to calculate the local context vector at current time step. The context vector c_t is then computed as a weighted sum of the annotations h_i:

$$c_i^l = \sum\nolimits_{j \in [p_i - D, p_i + D]} \alpha_{ij}^l h_i \tag{9}$$

It can be seen that the farther away from the center p_i, the lower the weight α_{ij}^l corresponding to source annotation at the position.

3   An Attention Mechanism Based on Syntactic Branch Distance

3.1   Syntactic Branch Distance

Dependency parsing is one of main methods for syntactic analysis. Its basic task is to determine the syntactic structure of a sentence or the interdependence of words in a sentence. Syntactic parsing determines whether the composition of an input sentence conforms to a given grammar, and constructs a syntax tree to represent the structure of the sentence and the relationship between the syntactic components of each level, that is, which words in a sentence constitute a phrase. The dependency syntax tree is a representation of dependency syntax analysis. The dominators and subordinates of dependent syntax tags in the dependent syntax tree are described as parent nodes and child nodes respectively. It expresses formal grammatical rules and constraints as points connected by trees and the information they carry, so that the dependent syntactic analysis of sentences is transformed into a task of finding a spatially connected structure or a set of dependent pairs of the sentence. In other words, it can well represent a sentence from the perspective of syntactic analysis, and resolve the internal relations among words in the sentence for acquiring sufficient information from the dependency tree. The syntax distance, the connecting distance of any two words in the tree, can be used to describe the close syntax relationship between words. We use Stanford parser[1], which is a Java open source parser based on probabilistic syntax analysis, to acquire dependency pairs between words of a given sentence and generate a dependent syntax tree accordingly.

Generally, the context vector of current time step is obtained by respectively aligning all the encoder states with alignment weights, and the decoder predicts the target word at the next time step by using the context vector. In the traditional attention mechanism, the alignment weight is given by the linear index distance of words in a source sentence. That is to say, in the sequential structure of a sentence, the smaller the index distance between a word and the current source word to be translated, the greater the alignment weight of the word, the greater the contribution it makes to target word prediction when the source word is translated. However, the use of linear index distance is not rigorous, since the linear distance only considers the order in which the words appear in the sentence but ignores the deep structure of the sentence, disregarding the syntactic structure of the sentence and the inter-word dependencies, including composition, context, etc. For example, the three words in Fig. 1, "gave", "went" and "fly" are in the same branch of a dependency tree, and the syntax distances between them are small, <"gave", "went", $d_{syntax} = 1$>, <"gave", "fly", $d_{syntax} = 2$>, <"went", "fly", $d_{syntax} = 1$>. These values indicate that the words have a close syntax relationship, but it is obvious that the linear index distance between them is large, <"gave", "went", $d_{linear} = 5$>, <"gave", "fly", $d_{linear} = 12$>, <"went", "fly ", $d_{linear} = 7$>. Meanwhile, the traditional attention mechanism is inclined to ignore these syntax connections, resulting in translation of the linearly adjacent but less syntax related words are set with greater alignment weights, while words that are more syntax-related and farther away in linear distance are set with less alignment weight, which cause some syntax errors during translation.

To address the mentioned problems, this paper introduces the prior knowledge of syntax tree based on the local attention, and make modifications to the commonly used syntax distances to proposed a new syntactic branch distance, for obtaining more accurate source sentence information when generating target words. Given a source sentence X with dependency tree T, each node represents a source word x_i. For source word as root node, since it has strong syntax relationship with all the words in the sentence, we compute the path length of all remaining words reaching the root word through tree T to obtain syntactic branch distance sequence of source word. That is, this calculates the effective context vector to translate the root node based on the encoder state of all source words and the weighted average of the alignment weights. For source

---

[1] https://nlp.stanford.edu/nlp.

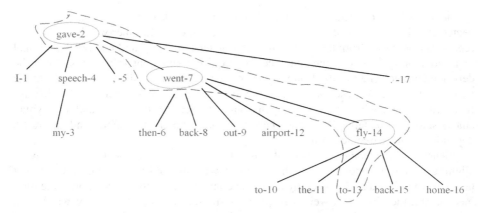

Fig. 1. An example of words in the same branch of a dependency tree

word in leaf node and internal node positions, according to whether the remaining words and current word are in the same branch on the tree T, two situations are considered. For words that are in the same branch, we define syntactic branch distance of the source word as the level deviations between other words and the source word in syntax tree. For words that are not in the same branch, we set the syntactic branch distance value to the depth of dependency tree of the sentence. The significance of this setting is firstly to reduce the influence of these words on different orders and inter-ference noise to the translated source words. Second, during the translation process, since there still convey many useful information in different branch words, it can be combined with the translated source words to form some phrases, so the empirical value is necessarily set to the depth of syntax tree. Therefore, unwanted noise words can be removed to some extent to ensure proper attention to the word on different branches. Generally, the words on the same branch of a dependency tree are highly correlated with their currently translated source words, thus corresponding alignment weights are large, while the words on other branches have relatively low alignment weights.

As shown in Fig. 2, the syntactic branch distance between the words "*affect*" and "*people*" is 2 for the source word is a root node. For a source word is in leaf node or internal node, the syntactic branch distance between the words "*these*" and "*people*" is 1, while syntactic branch distance between "*these*" and "*dangerous*" is 4 (depth of the dependency tree) for they are not in the same branch. Similarly, each word in the tree is traversed according to the order of source word and the corresponding syntactic branch distance sequence is computed. Finally, all sequences are combined into a syntactic branch distance mask matrix of the sentence. The obtained syntactic branch distance mask matrix is thus shown in Fig. 3.

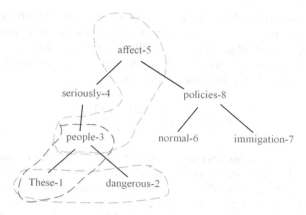

Fig. 2. The dependency syntax tree T and syntactic branch distance calculation for a given stentence (yellow dotted line denotes root nodes, while red and green lines denote the same branch and different branch in leaf and internal nodes, respectively) (Color figure online)

	These	dangerous	people	seriously	affect	normal	immigration	policies
These	0	h	1	2	3	h	h	h
dangerous	h	0	1	2	3	h	h	h
people	1	1	0	1	2	h	h	h
seriously	h	2	1	0	1	h	h	h
affect	3	3	2	1	0	2	2	1
normal	h	h	h	h	2	0	h	1
immigration	h	h	h	h	2	h	0	1
policies	h	h	h	h	1	1	1	0

Fig. 3. The syntactic branch distance mask matrix M of the sentence (Each line represents a syntactic branch distance mask for a source word, where h is the depth of syntax tree)

3.2 The Attention Mechanism Based on Tuned Branch Syntax Distance

In order to solve the problem of inaccurate focused source context of local attention, we propose an attention mechanism based on a new syntactic branch distance, aiming at integrating accurate and effective syntax knowledge with attention mechanism to improve the accuracy of source-side context information.

We use the seq2seq model framework, which mainly consists of a encoder model by a bidirectional RNN, a decoder model by a conditional RNN and a generator which depend on conditional probability. Besides, further improvement work is conducted in the attention mechanism. First, the alignment source position p_i is learned for each target word by the Eq. (7) at the current decoding time step i. After that, the alignment weights constrain by syntactic branch distance through source position p_i and syntactic branch distance matrix M are calculated using Eq. (10):

$$e_{ij}^{bs} = e_{ij} \exp\left(-\frac{(M_{[p_i][j]})2}{2\sigma^2}\right) \tag{10}$$

Furthermore, the standard deviation σ is set to $h/2$ in our experiments, where h is empirically set to be the depth of syntax tree of a given sentence and it is similar to the order of syntax tree level. First of all, the syntactic branch distance value of a word not in the same branch is set to be depth of dependency tree of the sentence. Secondly, all syntactic branch distances of words can be obtained from the hierarchy of a syntax tree. In order to remove unwanted noise words to some extent without losing proper attention to words on different branches, we set the largest syntactic branch distance to be the depth number of syntax tree.

l is the length of the sentence, and $\alpha_{ij}^{bs_n}$ is normalized considering all the syntactic branch distances of current source word, i.e., the row of syntactic branch distance mask corresponding to the current source word.

$$\alpha_{ij}^{bs_n} = \frac{\exp\left(e_{ij}^{bs}\right)}{\sum_{k \in M_{[p_i][k]} < h} \exp\left(e_{ik}^{bs}\right)}, j \in [0, l] \tag{11}$$

Finally, the context vector c_i^{bs} is calculated as the weighted sum of the source annotations of attention by the weights alignment of the attention of single grammar branch distance.

$$c_i^{bs} = \sum_j^J \alpha_{ij}^{bs_n} h_j \tag{12}$$

4 Experiments and Results

4.1 Expreiment Settings

To evaluate the effectiveness of our proposed model, the commonly applied standard dataset IWSLT 2017[2] is used as the evaluation dataset. 204936 dual-language sentences in English and German is used as training data. The supplementary dev2010 dataset is as the validation data set, and tst2010, tst2011, tst2012, tst2013, tst2014 are used as testing data sets.

---

[2] https://sites.google.com/site/iwsltevaluation2017/Dialogues-task.

We use a local attention proposed by Luong et al. [5] as a baseline method. The local attention is improved on the basis of global attention. The local attention mechanism selectively focuses on the context of a window in which current source word is located in, and considers that the context can benefit decoder on the prediction of next generated word. Experiments prove that it not only reduce the computational cost, but also outperforms global attention on translation performance in terms of BLEU score.

The NMT model used in the experiment is implemented based on Nematus codes by Sennrich et al. [16]. We use the Stanford parser (Chang et al. [17]) to generate dependency trees for source sentences. Our model limits the source and target vocabulary size to 50 K and the maximum training sentence length to 50. We randomly shuffle our training data set in each epoch. The batch size is 40, the word embedding dimension is 512-dimensions, the hidden layer dimension is 1024-dimensions, and the decoded beam size is 12. The default dropout technique in Nematus is used on all the layers (Hinton et al. [18]). Our NMT model choose ADADELTA as the optimizer (Zeiler et al. [15]), and trains about 400,000 small batches. It runs on a single GeForce GTX 1080 GPU for 2 days. The case-sensitive 4-gram NIST BLEU score (Papineni et al. [19]) is used as the evaluation metric.

4.2 The Results

The performance comparison of our model with the baseline is conducted and the results is shown as Table 1. From the table, the translation results of attention NMT based on the syntactic branch distance constraint (as SbdAtt) on the IWSLT 2017 testing dataset is 23.49. Compared with global attention (as GlobalAtt), our proposed LocalAtt-SBD has increased 1.61 BLEU points on average. This indicates that, compared with global attention focusing on global information, our method acquires more accurate context information during the translation process, which effectively improves translation performance.

Table 1. Results on EN-DE translation tasks of different attention mechanism

EN-DE	dev2010	tst2010	tst2011	tst2012	tst2013	tst2014	tst2015	avg
GlobalAtt	19.87	21.94	24.45	21.93	22.72	20.05	22.22	21.88
LocalAtt	20.31	21.05	22.56	20.69	22.11	19.36	21.22	21.04
SbdAtt	**22.67**	**24.00**	**25.29**	**22.54**	**25.02**	**21.42**	**23.55**	**23.49**

In terms of the baseline local attention (as LocalAtt), our proposed LocalAtt-BSD has increased by 2.45 BLEU points on average, demonstrating that our method can learn more source dependency information to effectively improve the translation performance of NMT. The proposed syntactic branch distance attention can capture more translation information than linear distance attention to improve word prediction.

5 Conclusion

This paper tried to integrate the prior knowledge of syntactic analysis with traditional attention mechanism to improve translation performance. An attention mechanism based on tuned branch syntax was proposed. Syntax-directed selective attention on the word associated with source word, including the cases of the same branch and different branch with the source word, was proposed for the predication of target words. Experiment results on the IWSLT2017 showed that the proposed model outperformed the local attention baseline method. In the future, we will extend the experiment to other languages (such as Chinese-English) to test the scalability of the model and the applicability on long sentences.

Acknowledgements. This work was supported by National Natural Science Foundation of China (No.61772146).

References

1. Kalchbrenner, N., Blunsom, P.: Recurrent continuous translation models. In: Proceedings of the 2013 Conference on Empirical Methods in Natural Language Processing, pp. 1700–1709 (2013)
2. Cho, K., Merrienboer, B.V., Gülçehre, Ç., Bougares, F., Schwenk, H., Bengio, Y.: Learning phrase representations using RNN encoder-decoder for statistical machine translation. arXiv preprint arXiv:1406.1078 (2014)
3. Sutskever, I., Vinyals, O., Le, Q.V.: Sutskever, I., et al.: Sequence to sequence learning with neural networks. In: Advances in Neural Information Processing Systems, pp. 3104–3112 (2014)
4. Bahdanau, D., Cho, K., Bengio, Y.: Neural machine translation by jointly learning to align and translate. arXiv preprint arXiv:1409.0473 (2015)
5. Luong, M.T., Sutskever, I., Le, Q.V., et al.: Addressing the rare word problem in neural machine translation. Bull. Univ. Agric. Sci. Vet. Med. Cluj-Napoca. Vet. Med. **27**(2), 82–86 (2014)
6. Tai, K.S., Socher, R., Manning, C.D.: Improved semantic representations from tree-structured long short-term memory networks. arXiv preprint arXiv:1503.00075 (2015)
7. Sennrich, R., Haddow, B.: Linguistic input features improve neural machine translation. In: Proceedings of the First Conference on Machine Translation, Berlin, Germany, pp. 83–91. ACL (2016)
8. Eriguchi, A., Tsuruoka, Y., Cho, K.: Learning to parse and translate improves neural machine translation. In: Proceedings of the 55th Annual Meeting of the Association for Computational Linguistics, Vancouver, Canada, pp. 72–78. ACL (2017)
9. Li, J., Xiong, D., Tu, Z., Zhu, M., Zhou, G.: Modeling source syntax for neural machine translation. In: Proceedings of the 55th Annual Meeting of the Association for Computational Linguistics, Vancouver, Canada, pp. 688–697. ACL (2017)
10. Wu, S., Zhang, D., Yang, N., Li, M., Zhou, M.: Sequence-to-dependency neural machine translation. In: Proceedings of the 55th Annual Meeting of the Association for Computational Linguistics (Volume 1), Vancouver, Canada, pp. 698–707 (2017)

11. Eriguchi, A., Hashimoto, K., Tsuruoka, Y.: Tree-to-sequence attentional neural machine translation. In: Proceedings of the 54th Annual Meeting of the Association for Computational Linguistics, Berlin, Germany, pp. 823–833 (2016)
12. Chen, H., Huang, S., Chiang, D., Chen, J.: Improved neural machine translation with a syntax-aware encoder and decoder. In: Proceedings of the 55th Annual Meeting of the Association for Computational Linguistics, Vancouver, Canada, pp. 1936–1945 (2017)
13. Wu, S., Zhou, M., Zhang, D.: Improved neural machine translation with source syntax. In: Proceedings of the Twenty Sixth International Joint Conference on Artificial Intelligence, IJCAI-2017, pp. 4179–4185 (2017)
14. Chen, K., Wang, R., Utiyama, M., Liu, L., Zhao, T., et al.: Neural machine translation with source dependency representation. In: Proceedings of the 2017 Conference on Empirical Methods in Natural Language Processing, Copenhagen, Denmark, pp. 23–32 (2017)
15. Zeiler M.D.: ADADELTA: an adaptive learning rate method. arXiv preprint arXiv:1212.5701 (2012)
16. Sennrich, R., Firat, O., Cho, K., et al.: Nematus: a toolkit for neural machine translation. In: Proceedings of the 15th Conference of the European Chapter of the Association for Computational Linguistics, Valencia, Spain, pp. 65–68 (2017)
17. Chang, P.C., Tseng, H., Jurafsky, D., Manning, C.D.: Discriminative reordering with Chinese grammatical relations features. In: Proceedings of the Third Workshop on Syntax and Structure in Statistical Translation, Boulder, Colorado, pp. 51–59 (2009)
18. Hinton, G., Srivastava, N., Krizhevsky, A., Sutskever, I., Salakhutdinov, R.: Improving neural networks by preventing co-adaptation of feature detectors. arXiv preprint arXiv:1207.0580 (2012)
19. Papineni, K., Roukos, S., Ward, T., Zhu, W.: BLEU: a method for automatic evaluation of machine translation. In: Proceedings of the 40th Annual Meeting of the Association for Computational Linguistics, Philadelphia, Pennsylvania, USA, pp. 311–318 (2002)
20. Wang, X., Pham, H., Yin, P., Neubig, G.: A tree-based decoder for neural machine translation. In: Proceedings of the 2018 Conference on Empirical Methods in Natural Language Processing, pp. 4772–4777(2018)
21. Ahmed, M., Samee, M. R., Mercer, R. E.: Improving tree-LSTM with tree attention. In: Proceedings of the 2019 IEEE 13th International Conference on Semantic Computing, pp. 247–254(2019)

Phrase-Based Chinese-Vietnamese Pseudo-Parallel Sentence Pair Generation

Jiaxin Zhai[1,2], Zhengtao Yu[1,2(✉)], Shengxiang Gao[1,2],
Zhenhan Wang[1,2], and Liuqing Pu[1,2]

[1] School of Information Engineering and Automation,
Kunming University of Science and Technology, Kunming 650500, China
ztyu@hotmail.com
[2] Artificial Intelligent Key Laboratory of Yunnan Province,
Kunming University of Science and Technology, Kunming 650500, China

Abstract. The lack of Chinese-Vietnamese parallel corpus has resulted in poor translation of Chinese-Vietnamese neural machine translation. In order to solve this problem, we propose a phrase-based Chinese-Vietnamese pseudo-parallel sentence pair generation method. This method expands the corpus of Chinese-Vietnamese neural machine translation and improves the performance of Chinese-Vietnamese neural machine translation. Firstly, based on the small-scale Chinese-Vietnamese parallel corpus, the method selects the phrase module according to the phrase syntactic structure information. Then this method combines word alignment information with replacement rules. Finally, the method achieves the expansion of Chinese-Vietnamese pseudo-parallel corpus. Experiments show that this method can effectively generate Chinese-Vietnamese pseudo-parallel sentence pairs and improve the performance of Chinese-Vietnamese neural machine translation.

Keywords: Phrase structure syntax · Phrase replacement · Pseudo-parallel sentence pair generation · Chinese-Vietnamese · Neural machine translation

1 Introduction

Neural mechanical translation can only achieve better results by training large-scale parallel corpora. Chinese-Vietnamese neural machine translation is a neural machine translation of resource scarcity types. It is difficult to obtain large-scale parallel corpus of Chinese-Vietnamese in a short time. Pseudo-parallel sentence pair generation is one of the important methods to extend pseudo-parallel corpus. Many researches have shown that pseudo-parallel corpora can also effectively improve the performance in neural machine translation of resource scarcity types.

There are three methods to generate pseudo-parallel corpora now. They are the method of back translation [1], the method of retelling [2–5], and the method of data augmentation [6]. These methods use a small amount of parallel corpus to generate pseudo-parallel corpora. But these specific methods are different. The back translation based method uses monolingual corpus resources to generate pseudo-parallel corpora in the iterative process of the neural machine translation model. The retelling based

© Springer Nature Singapore Pte Ltd. 2019
S. Huang and K. Knight (Eds.): CCMT 2019, CCIS 1104, pp. 58–68, 2019.
https://doi.org/10.1007/978-981-15-1721-1_6

method uses external resources to reproduce the bilingual parallel corpus. The method based on data enhancement uses the information of parallel corpus, and replaces the module under the certain rules to realize the generation of pseudo-parallel corpus.

The method based on data enhancement can achieve better results without introducing additional resources. Therefore, this paper uses the method of data enhancement to realize the generation of Chinese-Vietnamese pseudo-parallel corpora. This method is also called a phrase-based Chinese-Vietnamese pseudo-parallel sentence pair generation method. This method firstly realizes the word alignment and phrase syntactic structure analysis for small-scale Chinese-Vietnamese parallel corpus. Then the method extracts the Chinese-Vietnamese aligned noun phrase (NP) and verb phrase (VP) according to the word alignment information and the phrase syntactic structure information of the parallel sentence pair, and form a collection of Chinese-Vietnamese alignment phrases. Finally, according to the phrase syntactic parsing tree of the Chinese and Vietnamese parallel sentence pairs, we find the NP and VP structures at different depths. At the same time, we use the set of aligned phrases to replace the phrases in the sentence, and use the language model to verify the newly generated sentences, and finally generate the Chinese and Vietnamese pseudo-parallel sentence pairs.

2 Related Work

In recent years, domestic and foreign scholars have studied the methods of corpus generation for small-scale parallel corpora, and have achieved a series of results. On the premise of not introducing additional resources, He et al. [5] proposed a paraphrase method based on dependency analysis and sentence generation. The method obtains a dependency tree by performing dependency analysis on sentences, and then generates multiple natural language sentences from the dependency tree. The sentence generated by this method has no lexical change compared to the original sentence. However, this method has changed the word order and improved the quality of machine translation without introducing additional resources. Fadae et al. [6] proposed the method of TDA (Translation Data Augmentation) to generate pseudo-parallel sentence pairs. The method first replaces the common words in the parallel sentence pairs with the rare words, and obtains the pseudo-parallel sentence pairs. To ensure that the pseudo-parallel sentence pairs are grammatically and semantically correct, the method uses a language model to filter pairs the pseudo-parallel sentences pairs. The pseudo-parallel sentence pair through the screening mechanism is the training corpus that can be used as a neural machine translation. Cai et al. [7] use data enhancement technology to expand the training data of resource-starved languages. The method first blocks the sentence and then finds the two most similar modules in the sentence. Finally, by forming a new sentence by adjusting their position, we have realized the extension of the pseudo-parallel sentence pair.

These results have effectively expanded the scale of translation corpus and improved the performance of machine translation. He et al. [5] adjust the order of statistical machine translation by changing word order. Fadae et al. [6] and Cai et al. [7] did not consider sentence structure complexity when they use module substitution to generate pseudo-parallel corpora. This method leads to grammatical semantic errors in the sentence. We believe that the granularity of words is too small, and there is a one-to-many problem in the process of word alignment. Therefore, there will be grammatical and semantic errors in the sentence during the replacement process. There is also the problem that the replaced alignment words do not match in the sentence. The smallest translation unit is composed of multiple words. It is difficult to have a one-to-many problem. However, if we perform module replacement without the instruction of syntactic information, it is prone to grammatical errors.

In order to solve these problems, this paper proposes a phrase-based method for generating Chinese and Vietnamese pseudo-parallel sentence pairs. In this method, we use the phrase syntax structure information to guide the phrase replacement process. This approach not only avoids one-to-many problems, but also avoids syntactic errors in the replacement process.

3   Phrase-Based Extension Model of Chinese-Vietnamese Pseudo-Parallel Sentences

This section focuses on the Chinese and Vietnamese phrase extraction and alignment, as well as the phrase replacement rules. Figure 1 is the overall frame diagram of this document.

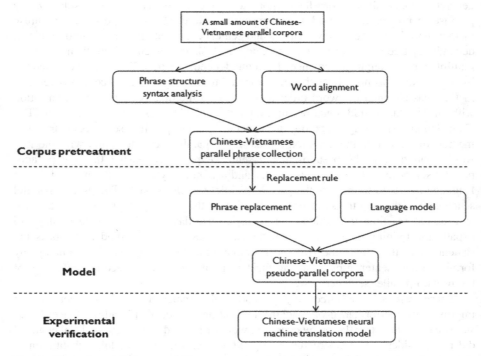

Fig. 1. Phrase-based Chinese and Vietnamese pseudo-parallel sentence pair generation model

3.1   Chinese-Vietnamese Sentence Structure

The main syntactic components of Chinese and Vietnamese are arranged in the same order, and the order of the modifiers is inconsistent in most cases. Modern linguistics has found that all languages in the world seem to have the same structure [8].

(1)   A sentence (ROOT) consists of at least one simple clause (IP);

$$ROOT \rightarrow IP^* \qquad (1)$$

(2)   A simple clause (IP) consists of a noun phrase (NP) and a verb phrase (VP);

$$IP \rightarrow NP\ VP \qquad (2)$$

(3)   A noun phrase (NP) is composed of the qualifier (det), the adjective (A), and the noun (N);

$$NP \rightarrow det\ A^*N \qquad (3)$$

(4)   A verb phrase (VP) consists of a noun phrase (NP) and a verb (V).

$$VP \rightarrow NP\ VP \qquad (4)$$

There are other phrase structures in Chinese and Vietnamese sentences, such as prepositional phrases (PP). This article mainly uses noun phrases (NP) and verb phrases (VP) as phrases. In particular, the noun phrase (NP) here has only one word.

3.2   Chinese-Vietnamese Phrase Alignment

There are not natural spacers between words in Chinese sentences. Although there are spaces in Vietnamese sentences. However, spaces are used as spacers for syllables. A syllable is probably not a separate word. We use Stanford University's Stanford NLP [9] toolkit for word segmentation and syntactic structure analysis of Chinese and Vietnamese corpora. At the same time, we use GIZA++ [10] to perform the Chinese-Vietnamese word alignment processing, and obtain the Chinese-Vietnamese word alignment information.

After the syntactic parsing of the Chinese-Vietnamese parallel sentence pairs, we can obtain the phrase syntactic structure tree of the parallel sentence pairs. Figure 2 (a) is a syntactic parse of the Chinese phrase structure syntax tree. Figure 2(b) is the corresponding Vietnamese phrase structure syntax tree. The phrase structure syntax tree of the Chinese and Vietnamese parallel sentence pairs is similar. Both the NP phrase and the VP phrase in the sentence are at the same depth in the tree, and the components that make up the phrases are similar.

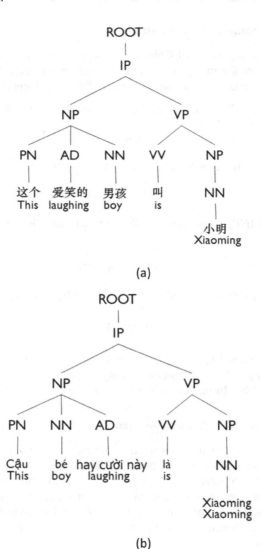

Fig. 2. Chinese and Vietnamese syntax tree.

Since the Chinese-Vietnamese parallel sentence pairs have similar syntax structures, we find all NP nodes and VP nodes in the tree. And we use each NP node and VP node as the root node to form multiple subtrees, each subtree is the phrase in this article. Then we use the word alignment information, the depth information of the node, and the node information of each subtree to perform the phrase alignment. Table 1 is the phrase after the alignment of the Chinese and Vietnamese parallel sentences.

For the phrase consisting of at least two words, we add it to the collection of Chinese and Vietnamese aligned phrases. For an NP phrase containing only one word, if the word is a rare word (the frequency of occurrence in the corpus is less than C), then we add this NP phrase block to the set of Chinese-Vietnamese aligned phrases.

Table 1. Alignment phrases in Chinese-Vietnamese parallel sentence pairs.

phrase	Chinese	Vietnamese
1	(NP(PN 这个(This))(AD 爱笑的 (laughing))(NN 男孩(boy)))	(NP(PN Cậu(This))(NN bé(boy))(AD hay cười này(laughing)))
2	(VP(VV 叫(is))(NP(NN 小明 (Xiaoming))))	(VP(VV là(is))(NP(NN Xiaoming (Xiaoming))))
3	(NP(NN 小明(Xiaoming)))	NP(NN Xiaoming(Xiaoming)))

3.3 Phrase Replacement

Phrase structure syntax analysis can transform sentences into tree structures. The structure of this tree puts the words in the right place, and the structure of the tree is modular [8]. In the phrase syntax tree, the noun phrase NP and the verb phrase VP are like the components of a certain shape. According to the rules of the phrase structure syntax tree, we can insert or replace one component (phrase) arbitrarily with another component (phrase).

Therefore, the rules for the replacement of phrases in this article are mainly:

(1) The same phrase can be replaced. That is, the NP phrase in the sentence can only be replaced with the NP phrase, and the VP phrase can only be replaced with the VP phrase.

(2) Each sentence replaces only one phrase at a time, and the new sentence pair no longer replaces the phrase.

This substitution rule can not only change the word frequency information of the corpus, but also change the structural information of the sentence. When we replace the other phrase blocks with a noun phrase consisting of only one rare word, we can increase the frequency of occurrence of rare words and enhance the generalization ability of rare words. When the phrases of different sizes are replaced, the structural information of the sentence is also changed.

Figure 3(a) is a phrase replacement for changing the word frequency information, and Fig. 3(c) is a phrase replacement for changing the syntax structure.

In Fig. 3(a), we also replace the NP phrase in the Chinese-Vietnamese parallel sentence with an NP phrase in the Chinese-Vietnamese aligned phrase set, which changes the corpus frequency information. In Fig. 3(b), we replace the NP phrase consisting of one word in a sentence with a more complex NP phrase, which changes the structural information of the sentence.

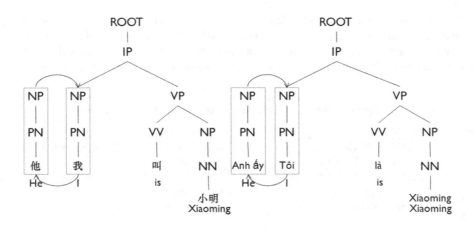

(a)

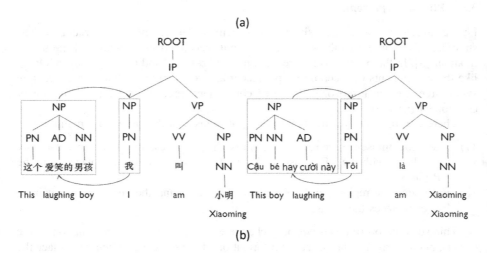

(b)

Fig. 3. The rules of phrase replacement

3.4   RNN-Based Language Model Verification Mechanism

We believe that the Chinese and Vietnamese sentence pairs generated under the guidance of the phrase structure syntax information have fewer grammatical errors, but many sentence pairs have semantic errors. In order to judge whether the Chinese and Vietnamese sentences obtained by phrase substitution conform to the grammatical and semantic features, we use the verification mechanism of the RNN-based language model. The verification mechanism can predict the probability of occurrence of the next word according to the context of the text, and can further calculate the probability of occurrence of the entire sentence. In theory, when the grammatical semantics of the corpus of the training language model is correct, sentences with wrong grammatical semantics will get lower scores.

In order to ensure that the generated Chinese-Vietnamese sentence pairs are correct in syntax and semantics, we constructed Chinese and Vietnamese language models for verification. The specific process is shown in Fig. 4.

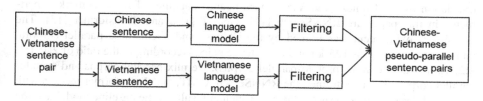

Fig. 4. Language model verification mechanism.

Figure 4 is the flow of the RNN-based language model verification mechanism. The Chinese language model and the Vietnamese language model were trained using Chinese Wikipedia corpus and Vietnamese Wikipedia corpus. For the generated Chinese-Vietnamese sentence pairs, we use the Chinese language model and the Vietnamese language model to score Chinese sentences and Vietnamese sentences. This score is the probability that a sentence will appear. If the score of the sentence is higher, it means that the higher the probability of the sentence appearing, the higher the probability that the sentence is correct in grammatical semantics. When the score of a sentence is less than the threshold we set, we think that the sentence is the wrong sentence, and filter out the sentence of the Chinese-Vietnamese sentences. Only when the Chinese sentences and Vietnamese sentences in the Chinese and Vietnamese sentences are screened by the language model, we use the Chinese and Vietnamese sentence pairs as the Chinese and Vietnamese pseudo-parallel corpus for training the Chinese and Vietnamese neural machine translation models.

For the selection of the language model threshold, we use the language model to score the monolingual corpus of the corresponding language, and separately calculate the lowest score in the monolingual corpus, which is used as the threshold of the corresponding language model.

4 Experiment

4.1 Data Settings

This paper is based on the small-scale parallel sentence pairs of Chinese and Vietnamese to generate Chinese-Vietnamese pseudo-parallel sentence pairs. Therefore, we will use the 120,000 Chinese-Vietnamese parallel sentence pairs crawled from the Internet as the sentence pairs to be expanded.

Before performing pseudo-parallel sentence pairs based on phrase substitution, we also need to perform a series of pre-processing work on Chinese-Vietnamese parallel corpus, including word segmentation, word alignment, phrase extraction, and phrase alignment.

4.2   Experimental Results

In this paper, we mix Chinese-Vietnamese parallel corpus with Chinese-Vietnamese pseudo-parallel corpus in different proportions. Through this approach, we verify the influence of the generated Chinese and Vietnamese pseudo-parallel corpus on the translation of the Chinese and Vietnamese neural machines. The benchmark experiments in this paper are RNNSearch [11], GNMT [12], and Transformer [13]. The benchmark experiment was trained by the Chinese and Vietnamese parallel corpora, and the corpus size was 125 k parallel sentence pairs. According to the ratio of 2:1, 1:1, 1:2, 1:5 (parallel corpus: pseudo-parallel corpus), we mix parallel corpus and pseudo-parallel corpus. Then we trained the RNNSearch, GMT, and Transformer models with the mixed corpus. Table 2 shows the experimental results of the baseline model and the addition of pseudo-parallel corpus. The evaluation index is the value of BLEU.

Table 2. Experimental results after adding pseudo-parallel corpus.

Mixed ratio (parallel: pseudo-parallel)	RNNSearch	GNMT	Transformer
–	13.43	14.21	18.63
2:1	13.86	14.49	18.86
1:1	14.08	14.83	19.15
1:2	14.70	15.20	19.63
1:5	14.55	15.57	20.06

After joining the Chinese-Vietnamese pseudo-parallel corpora, the performance of the Chinese and Vietnamese neuromachine translations has generally improved. For the RNNSearch model, when the mixing ratio of the Chinese-Vietnamese parallel corpus and the Chinese-Vietnamese pseudo-parallel corpus is 1:2, the value of the BLEU is the highest. For the GNMT model, when the mixing ratio of the Chinese-Vietnamese parallel corpus and the Chinese-Vietnamese pseudo-parallel corpus is 1:5, the value of the BLEU is the highest. For the Transformer model, when the mixing ratio of the Chinese-Vietnamese parallel corpus and the Chinese-Vietnamese pseudo-parallel corpus is 1:5, the value of the BLEU is the highest. In general, the more pseudo-parallel corpora generated by the method of this paper, the better the performance of Chinese-Vietnamese neural machine translation. Table 3 is a partial pseudo-parallel sentence pair generated by the phrase block replacement to generate pseudo-parallel sentence pairs.

From the experimental results, the generated Chinese-Vietnamese pseudo-parallel sentence pairs have higher quality. In the pseudo-parallel sentence pairs between Chinese-Vietnamese, there may be cases where Chinese and Vietnamese cannot be completely translated because of the word alignment. However, since this situation is rare, we believe that the generated Chinese-Vietnamese pseudo-parallel sentence pairs have higher quality.

Table 3. Pseudo-parallel sentence pair generation results based on phrase substitution.

Chinese	Vietnamese
这是西班牙的EUPHORE粉尘和烟雾研究实验室。(This is the EUPHORE dust and smoke research laboratory in Spain.)	ĐâylàPhòngnghiêncứukhóibụi EUPHORE ở Tây Ban Nha. (This is the EUPHORE dust and smoke research laboratory in Spain.)
这是西班牙的科学仪器。(This is the Spanish scientific instruments.)	Đâylàmộtcôngcụ khoa họctừTây Ban Nha. (This is the Spanish scientific instruments.)
这是西班牙的最大的科学会议。(This is the largest scientific conference in Spain.)	Đâylàhộinghị khoa họclớnnhất ở Tây Ban Nha. (This is the largest scientific conference in Spain.)
这是西班牙的头条新闻。(This is the headline news of Spain.)	Đâylà tin tứctiêuđềcủaTây Ban Nha. (This is the headline news of Spain.)
这是一场全球性的品牌推广活动。(This is a global branding event.)	Đâylàmộtsựkiệnthươnghiệutoàncầu. (This is a global branding event.)
这是我的第二本书。(This is my second book.)	Đâylàcuốnsáchthứhaicủatôi. (This is my second book.)
这是一场狩猎游戏吗? (Is this a hunting game?)	Đâycóphảimộttròsăntimkhông? (Is this a hunting game?)

5 Summary

This paper proposes a pseudo-parallel corpus generation method based on small-scale Chinese-Vietnamese parallel corpora. We transform the generation of pseudo-parallel corpus into the replacement and recombination of elements between sentences. We combine the noun phrase (NP) and the verb phrase (VP) in the phrase structure syntax tree into a phrase block. Then we reorganize the sentences based on the principle that phrases of the same nature can be replaced. Finally, we use the language model to grammatically and semantically constrain the newly generated sentences, and achieve the purpose of generating pseudo-parallel sentence pairs with correct grammatical semantics. The experimental results show that the proposed method can generate Chinese-Vietnamese pseudo-parallel corpus with high quality, which effectively improves the performance of Chinese-Vietnamese neural machine translation.

Acknowledgements. The work was supported by National key research and development plan project (Grant Nos. 2018YFC0830105, 2018YFC0830100), National Natural Science Foundation of China (Grant Nos. 61732005, 61672271, 61761026, and 61762056), Yunnan high-tech industry development project (Grant No. 201606), and Natural Science Foundation of Yunnan Province (Grant No. 2018FB104).

References

1. Sennrich, R., Haddow, B., Birch, A.: Improving Neural Machine Translation Models with Monolingual Data. arXiv preprint arXiv:1511.06709 (2015)
2. He, W., Zhao, S.Q., Wang, H.F., et al.: Enriching SMT training data via paraphrasing. In: Proceedings of the 5th International Joint Conference on Natural Language Processing (IJCNLP), 8–13 November 2011, Chiang Mai, Thailand, pp. 803–810 (2011)
3. Bond, F., Nichols, E., Appling, D.S., et al.: Improving statistical machine translation by paraphrasing the training data. In: Proceedings of the International Workshop on Spoken Language Translation (IWSLT), 20–21 October 2008, Honolulu, Hawaii, USA, pp. 150–157 (2008)
4. Nakov, P.: Improved statistical machine translation using monolingual paraphrases. In: Proceedings of the 18th European Conference on Artificial Intelligence (ECAI), 21–25 July 2008, Patras, Greece, pp. 338–342 (2008)
5. He, W., Liu, T.: Parse-realize based paraphrasing and SMT corpus enriching. J. Harbin Inst. Technol. **45**(5), 45–50 (2013)
6. Fadaee, M., Bisazza, A., Monz, C.: Data Augmentation for Low-Resource Neural Machine Translation. arXiv preprint arXiv:1705.00440 (2017)
7. Cai, Z.L., Yang, M.M., Xiong, D.Y.: Data augmentation for neural machine translation. J. Chin. Inf. Process. **32**(7) (2018)
8. Pinker, S.: The Language Instinct: How the Mind Creates Language, pp. 101–105. Penguin, UK (2003)
9. Manning, C.D., Mihai, S., John, B., et al.: The Stanford CoreNLP natural language processing toolkit. In: Proceedings of the 52nd Annual Meeting of the Association for Computational Linguistics (ACL), 22–27 June 2014, Baltimore, MD, USA, pp. 55–60 (2014)
10. Och, F.J.: Giza++: training of statistical translation models (2001). http://www.informatik. rwth-aachen.de/Colleagues/och/ software/GIZA++.html
11. Bahdanau, D., Cho, K., Bengio, Y.: Neural machine translation by jointly learning to align and translate (2014). arXiv:1409.0473
12. Wu, Y., Schuster, M., Chen, Z., et al.: Google's Neural Machine Translation System: Bridging the Gap between Human and Machine Translation. arXiv preprint arXiv: 1609.08144 (2016)
13. Vaswani, A., Shazeer, N., Parmar, N., et al.: Attention is all you need. In: Advances in Neural Information Processing Systems 30: Annual Conference on Neural Information Processing Systems 2017 (NISP), 4–9 December 2017, Long Beach, CA, USA, pp. 6000–6010 (2017)

Quality Estimation with Transformer and RNN Architectures

Yulin Zhang, Chong Feng[✉], and Hongzheng Li

School of Computer Science, Beijing Institute of Technology,
Beijing 100081, China
{yulinzhang, fengchong, lihongzheng}@bit.edu.cn

Abstract. The goal of China Conference on Machine Translation (CCMT 2019) Shared Task on Quality Estimation (QE) is to investigate automatic methods for estimating the quality of Chinese↔English machine translation results without reference translations. This paper presents the submissions of our team for the sentence-level Quality Estimation shared task of CCMT19. Considering the good performance of neural models in previous shared tasks of WMT, our submissions also include two neural-based models: one is Bi-Transformer which proposes the model as a feature extractor with a bidirectional transformer and then processes the semantic representations of source and the translation output with a Bi-LSTM predictive model for automatic quality estimation, and the other BiRNN architecture uses only two bi-directional RNNs (bi-RNN) with Gated Recurrent Units (GRUs) as encoders, and learns representation of the source and translation sentence pairs to predict the quality of translation outputs.

Keywords: Quality Estimation · Transformer · Translation evaluation

1 Introduction

Quality estimation (QE) refers to the task of measuring the quality of machine translation (MT) system outputs without reference to the gold translations (Blatz et al. 2004; Specia et al. 2013). QE can be performed on multiple granularities, including at word level, sentence level, or document level. QE results can be particularly useful during the costly Post-Edition (PE) process, the process of manually correcting MT output to achieve a publishable quality. QE indicates if an MT unit (i.e. a word, a phrase, a sentence, a paragraph or a document) is worth post-editing.

The QE task is usually cast as a supervised regression or classification task, with a rather small amount of manually annotated or/and post-edited data. This data can be labelled using automatic metrics towards post-edited references.

QE has been a shared task of WMT since 2012. Early work on this problem mainly focused on hand-crafted features with simple regression/classification models (Ueffing and Ney 2007; Bicici 2013). Traditional baseline models have two modules:

© Springer Nature Singapore Pte Ltd. 2019
S. Huang and K. Knight (Eds.): CCMT 2019, CCIS 1104, pp. 69–76, 2019.
https://doi.org/10.1007/978-981-15-1721-1_7

human-crafted rule-based feature extraction model via QuEst++[1] (Specia et al. 2015); and an SVM regression with an RBF kernel as well as grid search algorithms for predicting how much effort is needed to fix translations to acceptable results or a sequence-labeling model with CRFsuite toolkit[2] to predict which word in the translation output needs to be edited. A recently proposed predictor-estimator model with stack propagation (Kim et al. 2017) is a recurrent neural network (RNN) based feature extractor and quality prediction model that ranked first place in WMT17. Another novel method is to train an Automatic Post-Editing (APE) system and adapt it to predict sentence-level quality scores and word-level quality labels (Martins et al. 2017). Alibaba's system with Transformer architecture outweighs all other systems in the QE task of WMT 2018 (Wang et al. 2018).

This paper presents our submitted systems for Chinese-English and English-Chinese sentence-level QE tasks in CCMT2019. Which consists two neural models: one is Bi-Transformer QE and the other is Bi-RNN QE.

The Bi-Transformer QE has two phases: feature extraction and quality estimation. In the phase of feature extraction, it extracts high-level latent joint semantics and alignment information between the source and the translation output, relying on the "feature extractor" introduced by (Fan et al. 2018) as a prior knowledge model, which is trained on large-scale parallel corpus. The high-level latent semantic features exported from the prior knowledge model are fed into a predictive model in the phase of quality estimation, with which the scoring prediction for the sentence-level task.

The Bi-RNN QE architecture uses two bi-directional RNNs (bi-RNN) with Gated Recurrent Units (GRUs) as encoders to learn the representation of the source and translation sentence pair. The representations of the source and of the automatic translation are learned independently.

In the following sections, we will describe the two models in detail and conduct experiments for the task participation.

2   Systems Description

2.1   Bi-Transformer

The overall model architecture of the proposed Bi-Transformer is illustrated in Fig. 1. The Bi-Transformer QE contains two main modules: a feature extractor and a quality estimator.

Feature Extractor
The feature extractor extracts features representing latent semantic information of the source and translation pair. These features will be fed into the quality estimator to estimate the translation quality.

The feature extractor uses self-attention mechanism and transformer neural networks (Vaswani et al. 2017) to construct a bidirectional transformer architecture

---

[1] https://www.quest.dcs.shef.ac.uk/.

[2] www.chokkan.org/software/crfsuite/.

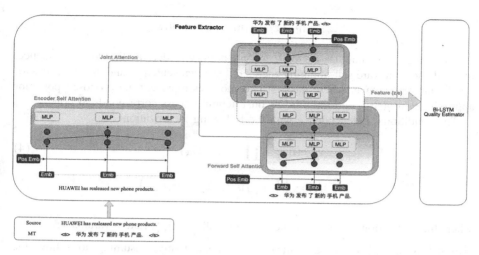

Fig. 1. Architecture of Bi-Transformer

(Fan et al. 2018), serving as a conditional language model. It is used to predict every single word in the target sentence given the entire source sentence and its context. The feature extractor consists of three sub-modules: the first is a transformer encoder for the source sentence, the second are forward and backward encoders for the target sentence with the masked self-attention in the transformer decoder module, and third is reconstruction for the target sentence. Once the feature extractor is fully trained, we can use the prior knowledge to extract the features for the subsequent translation quality estimator.

And the bi-directional LSTM (Graves and Schmidhuber 2005) is appropriate in the QE situation. Our system employs the feature extractor and the quality estimation based on Bi-LSTM.

Then, we will show the method to train the feature extractor with a parallel corpus including source and target sentence (s, t) pairs. According to the Bayes rule, we can write the posterior distribution of the latent variable as follow:

$$p(z|t,s) = \frac{p(t|z,s)p(z|s)}{p(t|s)} \tag{1}$$

where s represents the tokens sequence of source sentence, t for target sentence, and z is the latent variable to represent the encoded source sentence. Because the integral $p(t|s) = \int p(t|z)p(z|s)dz$ is usually intractable, we propose a variational distribution $q(z|t,s)$ to approximate true posterior by minimizing exclusive Kullback-Leibler (KL) divergence. We maximize the following function:

$$max\mathbb{E}_{q(z|t,s)}[p(t|z)] - D_{KL}(q(z|t,s)||p(z|s)) \tag{2}$$

In analogous to most VAE models (Kingma and Welling 2013), the expected log-likelihood is commonly approximated by a practical surrogated term:

$$\mathbb{E}_{q(z|t,s)}[p(t|z)] \approx p(t|\tilde{z}), \tilde{z} \sim q(z|t,s) \qquad (3)$$

There are three modules in total, self-attention encoder for the source sentence, forward and backward self-attention encoders for target sentence, and the reconstructor for the target sentence, where the first two modules represent the proposed posterior approximation $q(z|s,t)$ and the third reconstruction process corresponds to $p(t|z)$.

The conditional independence with the following factorization:

$$p(t|z) = \prod_k p(t_k|\vec{z}_k, \overleftarrow{z}_k) \qquad (4)$$

$$p(z|s,t) = \prod_k q(\vec{z}_k|s, t_{<k}) q\left(\overleftarrow{z}_k|s, t_{>k}\right) \qquad (5)$$

where the bidirectional latent variable z includes all $\left\{\vec{z}_k, \overleftarrow{z}_k\right\}$. Latent variables $\vec{z}_k$, $\overleftarrow{z}_k$ are sampled from $q(\vec{z}_k|s, t_{<k})$ and $q(\overleftarrow{z}_k|s, t_{>k})$ respectively, assuming to follow the Gaussian distribution. The latent representation $z_k = Concat\left(\vec{z}_k, \overleftarrow{z}_k\right)$, the entire latent variable is z. The embedding concatenation of two neighbor tokens is $Concat\left(e_{t_{k-1}}, e_{t_{k+1}}\right)$.

Quality Estimator

As for the Bi-LSTM Quality Estimator part, the sentence-level score prediction can be formulated as a regression problem with the objective function:

$$\vec{h}_{1:T}, \overleftarrow{h}_{1:T} = Bi - LSTM(\{f_k\}_{k=1}^T) \qquad (6)$$

$$\arg min\|h - sigmoid(w^T[\vec{h}_T; \overleftarrow{h}_T])\|_2^2 \qquad (7)$$

where $\vec{h}_T$ and $\overleftarrow{h}_T$ are the hidden states of the last time stamps of the Bi-LSTM's output, h represents the translation score (HTER) and w is a vector, and $f_k = Concat\left(\vec{z}_k, \overleftarrow{z}_k, e_{t_{k-1}}, e_{t_{k+1}}\right)$ is the extracted features from feature extractor for QE training data (s, m).

2.2 Bi-RNN

The proposed Bi-RNN QE system employs two bi-directional RNNs as encoders to learn the representation of the (source, MT) sentence pairs. A bi-RNN typically calculates a forward sequence of hidden states $(\vec{h}_1, \ldots, \vec{h}_J)$, and a backward sequence of hidden states $(\overleftarrow{h}_1, \ldots, \overleftarrow{h}_J)$. The hidden states $\vec{h}_j$ and $\overleftarrow{h}_j$ are concatenated to obtain the resulting representation h_j. In our approach, source and MT bi-RNNs are trained independently, as illustrated in Fig. 2.

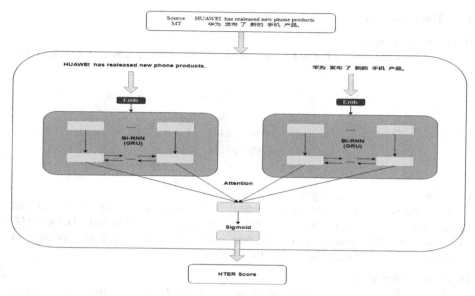

Fig. 2. Architecture of Bi-RNN

The two representations are then combined via concatenation. However, sentence-level QE scores reflect some importance of words within a sentence. Thus, weights should be applied to those representations. Such weighting is provided by the attention mechanism.

$$\alpha_j = \frac{\exp\left(W_a h_j^T\right)}{\sum_{k=1}^{J} \exp\left(W_a h_k^T\right)} \tag{8}$$

The resulting sentence vector is thus a weighted sum of word vectors: $v = \sum_{j=1}^{J} \alpha_j h_j$. A sigmoid output layer takes this vector as input and produces real-value quality scores.

3   Experiments

We submit the systems to sentence-level QE tasks in Chinese-English (C-E) and English-Chinese (E-C). In this part, we will provide a detailed description of the datasets together with the results for our submitted systems for each of these tasks.

3.1   Data Settings

Data for the Tasks
Table 1 shows the official dataset provided by CCMT 2019 sentence-level QE tasks.

Table 1. Data for CCMT 2019 sentence-level QE tasks

Task	Training	Dev	Test
C-E	10070	1143	1384
E-C	14789	1381	1444

Data for Bi-Transformer System
To train the feature extractor in the system of Bi-Transformer, we use the official parallel corpus released for the CWMT2018 Machine Translation task, *Datum2017*, which includes 1M sentence pairs. We then filtered the corpus with the criteria that length of sentences is equal to or less than 80.

Implementation Details
For Bi-Transformer system, the number of layers for the self-attention encoder and forward/backward self-attention decoder are all set as 2, where we use 8-head self-attention in practice. The number of hidden units for feed-forward sub-layer is 512. The feature exactor is trained on 4 TITAN Xp GPUs for about 1.5 days until convergence. For translation QE model, we use Bi-LSTM with one layer, and it is trained on 1 TITAN Xp GPU.

For Bi-RNN system, we use Gated Recurrent Units (GRUs) (Cho et al. 2014) as RNNs, and the following hyperparameters: word embedding dimensionality = 300, vocabulary size = 30K, size of the hidden units of the encoder = 50. The model is trained to minimize the mean squared error loss using the Adadelta optimizer (Zeiler 2012) on 1 GTX 1080 GPU.

3.2   Data Preprocessing

The data are preprocessed before training the models. Chinese sentences are word segmented with HanLP toolkit[3] and English data are tokenized with tokenizer tool[4] in the Moses decoder.

3.3   Evaluation Results

In order to compare the performance, we train both character-based and word-based models for each submitted system for the tasks. and Pearson's correlation coefficient is used as the primary evaluation metric to estimate the quality of prediction.

---

[3] https://github.com/hankcs/HanLP.

[4] https://github.com/moses-smt/mosesdecoder/tree/master/scripts/tokenizer.

As the organizers have not provided the gold labels for the test set, we can only obtain the results from the dev sets, as shown in Table 2.

Table 2. Evaluation results of our systems on dev set

System	Training	C-E(r)	E-C(r)
Bi-Transformer	Character-based	0.319	0.227
	Word-based	0.317	0.237
Bi-RNN	Character-based	0.296	0.229
	Word-based	0.310	0.240

As shown in above table, in C-E QE task, performance of Bi-Transformer are better than Bi-RNN under character-based and word-based setting. Inside the Bi-Transformer model, both the two settings have almost the same results. For another model, word-based setting achieves 0.02 higher than character-based. Meanwhile, in E-C direction, Bi-RNN slightly outperforms Bi-Transformer, and both word-based settings are higher than character-based inside the two models. In a word, except the character-based Bi-Transformer in C-E task, all the results of other word-based training are better than those of character-based.

From the translation directions, both systems for C-E are all better than those for E-C under the same training setting, which is consistent with the results of QE tasks for Chinese↔English in last year's CWMT.

4 Conclusion

This paper introduces our submissions to the sentence-level Quality Estimation tasks for Chinese-English and English-Chinese in CCMT 2019. We proposed two models named Bi-Transformer and Bi-RNN with both character-based and word-based training setting. Both the two systems are competitive in the QE tasks, but considering its simplicity and independence from external resources, as well as less training time, Bi-RNN may be more suitable for certain scenarios such as low-resource languages.

In the future, we plan to train the systems with larger size of corpus, and incorporate pretrained (contextual) embeddings and cross-lingual embeddings with the NMT module in the systems.

Acknowledgment. This work is supported by China Postdoctoral Science Foundation (CPSF, Grant No. 2018M640069).

References

Bicici, E.: Referential translation machines for quality estimation. In: Proceedings of the Eighth Workshop on Statistical Machine Translation, Sofia, Bulgaria, pp. 343–351 (2013)

Blatz, J., Fitzgerald, E., Foster, G., et al.: Confidence estimation for machine translation. In: Proceedings of the 20th International Conference on Computational Linguistics, p. 315 (2004)

Cho, K., van Merrienboer, B., Gulcehre, C., et al.: Learning phrase representations using RNN encoder-decoder for statistical machine translation. In: Proceedings of the 2014 Conference on Empirical Methods in Natural Language Processing (EMNLP), Doha, Qatar, pp. 1724–1734 (2014)

Fan, K., Li, B., Zhou, F., Wang, J.: "Bilingual expert" can find translation errors. arXiv preprint. arXiv:1807.09433 (2018)

Graves, A., Schmidhuber, J.: Frame-wise phoneme classification with bidirectional LSTM and other neural network architectures. Neural Netw. **18**(5–6), 602–610 (2005)

Kim, H., Lee, J.-H., Na, S.-H.: Predictor-estimator using multilevel task learning with stack propagation for neural quality estimation. In: Proceedings of the Second Conference on Machine Translation, Copenhagen, Denmark, pp. 562–568 (2017)

Martins, A.F.T., Kepler, F., Monteiro, J.: Unbabel's participation in the WMT17 translation quality estimation shared task. In: Proceedings of the Second Conference on Machine Translation, Copenhagen, Denmark, pp. 569–574 (2017)

Specia, L., Shah, K., Souza, J.G.C., Cohn, T.: QuEst-a translation quality estimation framework. In: Proceedings of the 51st Annual Meeting of the Association for Computational Linguistics: System Demonstrations, Sofia, Bulgaria, pp. 79–84 (2013)

Specia, L., Paetzold, G., Scarton, C.: Multi-level translation quality prediction with QuEst++. In: Proceedings of ACL 2015, Beijing, China, pp. 115–120 (2015)

Ueffing, N., Ney, H.: Word-level confidence estimation for machine translation. Comput. Linguist. **33**(1), 9–40 (2007)

Wang, J., Fan, K., Li, B., et al.: Alibaba submission for WMT18 quality estimation task. In: Proceedings of the Third Conference on Machine Translation, Brussels, Belgium, pp. 822–828 (2018)

Vaswani, A.., Shazeer, N., Parmar, N., et al.: Attention is all you need. In: Advances in Neural Information Processing Systems, pp. 5998–6008 (2017)

Zeiler, M.D.: ADADELTA: an adaptive learning rate method. arXiv:1212.5701 (2012)

NICT's Machine Translation Systems for CCMT-2019 Translation Task

Kehai Chen, Rui Wang[✉], Masao Utiyama, and Eiichiro Sumita

National Institute of Information and Communications Technology, Kyoto, Japan
{khchen,wangrui,mutiyama,eiichiro.sumita}@nict.go.jp

Abstract. This paper describes the NICT's neural machine translation systems for Chinese↔English directions in the CCMT-2019 shared news translation task. We used the provided parallel data augmented with a large quantity of back-translated monolingual data to train state-of-the-art NMT systems. We then employed techniques that have been proven to be most effective, such as fine-tuning, and model ensembling, to generate the primary submissions of Chinese↔English translation tasks.

Keywords: Neural machine translation · CCMT-2019 · NICT

1 Introduction

This paper presents the neural machine translation (NMT) systems built for National Institute of Information and Communications Technology (NICT)'s participation in the CCMT-19 shared News Translation Task for Chinese↔English directions. Specifically, we used the Transformer architecture to build our translation systems. We then employed techniques that have been proven to be most effective, such as back-translation, fine-tuning, and model ensembling, to generate the primary submissions of Chinese↔English translation tasks. All of our systems are constrained, i.e., we used only the parallel and monolingual data provided by the organizers to train and tune our systems. This system is also a part of our system for WMT19 [1][1].

The remainder of this paper is organized as follows. In Sect. 2, we present the data preprocessing. In Sect. 3, we introduce the details of our NMT systems. Empirical results obtained with our systems are analyzed in Sect. 4 and we conclude this paper in Sect. 5.

2 Datasets

2.1 Data

As parallel data to train our systems, we used all the provided parallel data for all our targeted translation directions. The training data for the Chinese↔English

---

[1] The Chinese-English task is jointly held by CCMT-2019 and WMT19. Therefore, part of these two system description papers are overlapped.

© Springer Nature Singapore Pte Ltd. 2019
S. Huang and K. Knight (Eds.): CCMT 2019, CCIS 1104, pp. 77–81, 2019.
https://doi.org/10.1007/978-981-15-1721-1_8

(ZH↔EN) translation tasks consists of two parts: (1) we selected the first 10 million lines of the News Crawl 2018 English corpus according to the finding of [6,11], (2) the corresponding synthetic data was generated through back-translation [5,8].

2.2   Pre-processsing

We applied tokenizer and truecaser of Moses [4] to the English sentences. For Chinese, we used Jieba[2] for tokenization but did not perform truecasing. For cleaning, we filtered out sentences longer than 80 tokens in the training data by using Moses script clean-n-corpus.perl, and replaced characters forbidden by Moses. Tables 1 and 2 present the statistics of the parallel and monolingual data, respectively, after pre-processing.

Table 1. Statistics of our pre-processed parallel data

Language pair	#Sentence pairs	#Tokens	
		Chinese	English
Chinese↔English	24.8M	509.9M	576.2M

Table 2. Statistics of our pre-processed monolingual data

Language	#Sentences	#Tokens
English	338.7M	7.5B
Chinese	130.5M	2.3B

3   MT Systems

3.1   NMT

We used Marian toolkit [2][3] to build competitive NMT systems based on the Transformer [10] architecture. We used the byte pair encoding (BPE) algorithm [9] for obtaining the sub-word vocabulary whose size was set to 50,000. The number of dimensions of all input and output layers was set to 512, and that of the inner feed-forward neural network layer was set to 2048. The number of attention heads in each encoder and decoder layer was set to eight. During training, the value of label smoothing was set to 0.1, and the attention dropout and residual dropout were set to 0.1. The Adam optimizer [3] was used to tune the parameters of the model. The learning rate was varied under a warm-up strategy with warm-up steps of 16,000. We validated the model with an interval

---

[2] https://github.com/fxsjy/jieba.
[3] https://marian-nmt.github.io.

of 5,000 batches on the development set and selected the best model according to BLEU [7] score on the development set. All our NMT systems were consistently trained on 4 GPUs,[4] with the following parameters for `Marian` (Table 3):

Table 3. Parameters for training `Marian`.

```
--type transformer  --max-length
100  --transformer-dim-ffn  4096
--dim-vocabs  50000  50000  -w  12000
--mini-batch-fit  --valid-freq 5000
--save-freq 5000 --disp-freq 500
--valid-metrics  ce-mean-words  perplexity
translation  --quiet-translation
--sync-sgd --beam-size  12
--normalize=1  --valid-mini-batch
16  --keep-best  --early-stopping
20 --cost-type=ce-mean-words
--enc-depth 6 --dec-depth 6
--tied-embeddings  --transformer-dropout
0.1 --label-smoothing  0.1
--learn-rate  0.0003 --lr-warmup  16000
--lr-decay-inv-sqrt  16000 --lr-report
--optimizer-params  0.9  0.98  1e-09
--clip-norm  5  --exponential-smoothing
```

3.2   Back-Translation of Monolingual Data

The so-called "back-translation" of monolingual has been shown to be one of the most efficient ways to exploit monolingual data for NMT [8]. It is simply to translate target monolingual data into the source language, using a pre-trained target-to-source NMT models, in order to produce a new synthetic parallel data that can be used to train NMT models. We concatenated the resulting synthetic parallel data to the original parallel data to train better NMT models. For En→Zh, we back-translated the entire XMU Chinese monolingual corpus containing 5.4M sentences as the source to produce synthetic English data. For Zh→En, we empirically compared the impact of back-translating different sizes of English monolingual data, using the first 10M lines of the concatenation of News Crawl-2016 and News Crawl-2017 English corpora to produce synthetic Chinese data.

3.3   Fine-Tuning and Ensemble of NMT Models

After the back-translation, we performed the training run independently for five times on the mixture of the original parallel data and the pseudo-parallel

---

[4] NVIDIA® Tesla® P100 16 Gb.

data, and thus obtain the translation models. The new model was further fine-tuned on the ccmt2018_newstest set for 20 epochs. Finally, we decoded the ccmt2019_newstest set with an ensemble of the five fine-tuned models to generate the primary submissions for the ZH↔EN tasks.

4   Results

Our systems are evaluated on the WMT2019NewsTest test set[5] for ZH↔EN tasks and the results are shown in Table 4. For EN→ZH, BLEU scores were computed on the basis of character-based segmentation. "w/backtr" and "w/o backtr" indicate with and without back-translation, respectively. "w/ft" indicates that this single model was fine-tuned on the ccmt2018_newstest sets. "ensemble" indicates that five fine-tuned single models were ensembled at decoding time.

Table 4. Results (BLEU-cased) of our MT systems on the ccmt2018_newstest test set.

System	ZH→EN	EN→ZH
Single model (w/o backtr)	23.3	30.3
Single model (w/backtr)	25.3	31.8
Single model (w/ft)	27.5	33.1
Five fine-tuned single models (ensemble)	31.0	34.5

Our observations from Table 4 are as follows: It is obvious that the back-translation, fine-tuning, and ensemble methods are greatly effective for the ZH↔EN tasks. In particular, the ensemble gave more improvements on the ZH→EN task over the "Single model+back-translation+fine-tuning" model than the EN→ZH task.

5   Conclusion

We presented in this paper the NICT's participation in the CCMT-2019 shared Chinese↔English news translation task. Our primary submissions to the tasks were the results of a simple combination of back-translation, fine-tuning, and ensemble methods. Our results confirmed that these three methods can incrementally improve translation performance of the Transformer NMT.

Acknowledgments. We are grateful to the anonymous reviewers and the area chair for their insightful comments and suggestions. Rui Wang was partially supported by JSPS grant-in-aid for early-career scientists (19K20354): "Unsupervised Neural Machine Translation in Universal Scenarios" and NICT tenure-track researcher startup fund "Toward Intelligent Machine Translation".

---

[5] http://www.statmt.org/wmt19/translation-task.html.

References

1. Dabre, R., et al.: NICT's supervised neural machine translation systems for the WMT19 news translation task. In: Proceedings of the Fourth Conference on Machine Translation (Volume 2: Shared Task Papers, Day 1), Association for Computational Linguistics, Florence, Italy, pp. 168–174, August 2019. https://www.aclweb.org/anthology/W19-5313

2. Junczys-Dowmunt, M., et al.: Marian: fast neural machine translation in C++. In: Proceedings of ACL 2018, System Demonstrations, Melbourne, Australia, pp. 116–121 (2018). http://aclweb.org/anthology/P18-4020

3. Kingma, D.P., Ba, J.: Adam: a method for stochastic optimization. CoRR abs/1412.6980 (2014). http://arxiv.org/abs/1412.6980

4. Koehn, P., et al.: Moses: open source toolkit for statistical machine translation. In: Proceedings of the 45th Annual Meeting of the Association for Computational Linguistics Companion Volume Proceedings of the Demo and Poster Sessions, Prague, Czech Republic, pp. 177–180 (2007). http://aclweb.org/anthology/P07-2045

5. Marie, B., et al.: NICT's unsupervised neural and statistical machine translation systems for the WMT19 news translation task. In: Proceedings of the Fourth Conference on Machine Translation (Volume 2: Shared Task Papers, Day 1), Association for Computational Linguistics, Florence, Italy, pp. 294–301, August 2019. https://www.aclweb.org/anthology/W19-5330

6. Marie, B., Wang, R., Fujita, A., Utiyama, M., Sumita, E.: NICT's neural and statistical machine translation systems for the WMT18 news translation task. In: Proceedings of the Third Conference on Machine Translation: Shared Task Papers, Belgium, Brussels, pp. 449–455, October 2018. https://www.aclweb.org/anthology/W18-6419

7. Papineni, K., Roukos, S., Ward, T., Zhu, W.J.: Bleu: a method for automatic evaluation of machine translation. In: Proceedings of 40th Annual Meeting of the Association for Computational Linguistics, Association for Computational Linguistics, Philadelphia, Pennsylvania, USA, pp. 311–318, July 2002. https://doi.org/10.3115/1073083.1073135, http://www.aclweb.org/anthology/P02-1040

8. Sennrich, R., Haddow, B., Birch, A.: Improving neural machine translation models with monolingual data. In: Proceedings of the 54th Annual Meeting of the Association for Computational Linguistics (Volume 1: Long Papers), Berlin, Germany, pp. 86–96 (2016). http://aclweb.org/anthology/P16-1009

9. Sennrich, R., Haddow, B., Birch, A.: Neural machine translation of rare words with subword units. In: Proceedings of the 54th Annual Meeting of the Association for Computational Linguistic, Berlin, Germany, pp. 1715–1725 (2016). http://aclweb.org/anthology/P16-1162

10. Vaswani, A., et al.: Attention is all you need. In: Guyon, I., et al. (eds.) Advances in Neural Information Processing Systems, vol. 30 (2017). https://papers.nips.cc/paper/7181-attention-is-all-you-need.pdf

11. Wang, R., Marie, B., Utiyama, M., Sumita, E.: NICT's corpus filtering systems for the WMT18 parallel corpus filtering task. In: Proceedings of the Third Conference on Machine Translation: Shared Task Papers, Association for Computational Linguistics, Belgium, Brussels, pp. 963–967, October 2018. https://doi.org/10.18653/v1/W18-6489, https://www.aclweb.org/anthology/W18-6489

NiuTrans Submission for CCMT19 Quality Estimation Task

Ziyang Wang[1], Hui Liu[1], Hexuan Chen[1], Kai Feng[1], Zeyang Wang[1], Bei Li[1],
Chen Xu[1], Tong Xiao[1,2(✉)], and Jingbo Zhu[1,2]

[1] NLP Lab, Northeastern University, Shenyang, China
{wangziyang,huiliu,chenhexuan,fengkai,wangzeyang,
libeinlp,xuchen}@stumail.neu.edu.cn
[2] NiuTrans Co., Ltd., Shenyang, China
{xiaotong,zhujingbo}@mail.neu.edu.cn

Abstract. This paper describes our system submitted for the CCMT 2019 Quality Estimation (QE) Task, including sentence-level and word-level. We propose a new method based on predictor-estimator architecture [7] in this task. For the predictor, we adopt Transformer-DLCL [17] (dynamic linear combination of previous layers) as our feature extracting models. In order to obtain the information of translations in both directions, we use right-to-left and left-to-right two models, concatenate two feature vectors as whole quality feature vectors. For the estimator, we use a multi-layer bi-directional GRU to predict HTER scores or OK/BAD labels for different tasks. We pre-train the predictor according to machine translation (MT) method with bilingual data from WMT2019 EN-ZH task, and then jointly train predictor and estimator with the QE task data. We also construct 50K pseudo data in different methods in respond to the data scarcity. The final system integrates multiple single models to generate results.

Keywords: Quality estimation · Deep Transformer · Bi-GRU

1 Introduction

Quality estimation (QE) refers to the task of evaluating the quality of MT results without any human annotated references [2]. We participate the CCMT 2019 QE task in both EN→ZH and ZH→EN directions. Each of them consists of two subtasks: word-level and sentence-level. Word level task is to predict OK/BAD labels for each word and gap in translation results, corresponding to mistranslation, over-translation and under-translation. Sentence-level task is to predict the Human-targeted Translation Edit Rate (HTER) scores [14] which represent the overall quality of the translation results.

In early works, human-crafted features were wildly used. A typical framework was QUEST++ [15] which provided a variety of features and machine learning methods to build QE models. In recent years, neural models significantly improved the performance in this task. Kim et al. [7] proposed a neural

© Springer Nature Singapore Pte Ltd. 2019
S. Huang and K. Knight (Eds.): CCMT 2019, CCIS 1104, pp. 82–92, 2019.
https://doi.org/10.1007/978-981-15-1721-1_9

network architecture called predictor-estimator, which adopted a bilingual recurrent neural network (RNN) language model [9] as predictor to extract feature vectors, and used a bidirectional RNN as estimator to predict QE scores. Fan et al. [5] introduced a bidirectional Transformer based pre-trained model for feature extraction, and used 4-dimensional mis-matching features from this model to improve performance.

In our work, all the tasks we submit share the same model architecture based on the predictor-estimator. We pre-train left-to-right and right-to-left deep Transformer models with a large amount of bilingual data as predictor. Byte-pair-encoding (BPE) [12] tokenization is applied to reduce the number of unknown tokens. After that, a multi-layer Bi-GRU is used as estimator, and is jointly trained with predictors using the quality estimation task data. We transform word-level tasks into binary classification problems and sentence-level tasks into regression problems for estimator model to predict labels or scores with the feature information extracted by predictor.

To further improve the performance of the predictor, we use target-side monolingual data to construct pseudo-data by various back-translation [3] methods, including beam search, sampling and sampling-topk [4]. Due to the scarcity of QE data, we also construct QE pseudo data. We regard real target-side sentences in bilingual data as personal edited results, and use beam search, sampling or sampling-topk to construct machine translation results. Finally, we used the TER tool [14] to generate word-level OK/BAD labels or sentence-level HTER scores.

Our system also employs the ensemble strategy to further improve model performance. By training multiple sub-models, the final results are fused by voting or averaging in different tasks.

2   Deep Transformer

A strong and effective feature extraction model is essential for the estimator to make more accurate predictions. We choose the pre-trained machine translation model to extract features. Neural Machine Translation (NMT) based on multilayer self-attention has shown strong results in many machine translation tasks. In order to improve the performance of machine translation and extract the information contained in the sentences more fully, we apply the structure of Pre-norm Transformer-DLCL. In this section, we describe the details about our deep architecture as below:

Pre-norm Transformer: For Transformer [16], learning deeper networks [1] is not easy because of the difficulty to optimize due to the gradient vanishing/exploring problem. But in recent implementations, Wang et al. [17] emphasized that the location of layer normalization [8] plays a vital role when training deep Transformer. In early versions of Transformer, layer normalization is placed after the element-wise residual addition. While in recent implementations, layer normalization is applied to the input of every sublayer, which can provide a direct way to pass error gradient from top to bottom. In this way pre-norm

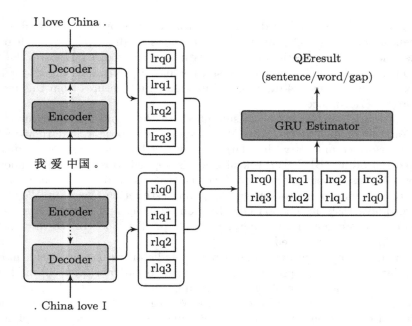

Fig. 1. The architecture of our model based on predictor-estimator.

Transformer is more efficient for training than post-norm (vanilla Transformer) when the model goes deeper.

Transformer-DLCL: In addition, a dynamic linear combination of previous layers method [17] was used in Transformer model. Transformer-DLCL employed direct links with all previous layers and offered efficient access to lower-level representations in a deep stack. An additional weight matrix $W_{l+1} \in R^{L \times L}$ was used to weight each incoming layer in a linear manner. This method can be formulated as:

$$\Psi(y_0, y_1 \ldots y_l) = \sum_{k=0}^{l} W_k^{l+1} LN(y_k) \tag{1}$$

Equation 1 provided a way to learn preference of layers in different levels of the stack, $\Psi(y_0, y_1 \ldots y_l)$ was the combination of previous layer representation. Furthermore, this method is model architecture free which can be integrated with either pre-norm Transformer or relative position Transformer [13] for further enhancement. The details can be seen in Wang et al. [17].

We used Transformer-DLCL model with 25 layers in encoder, and show the performance improvement of Transformer-DLCL vs. Transformer-base and Transformer-Big in Table 1.

Table 1. BLEU score and $\triangle$ BLEU [%] on WMT ZH→EN and EN→ZH *newstest2017.*

Task	Model	BLEU	$\triangle$BLEU
ZH→EN	Transformer-Base	26.58	–
	Transformer-Big	27.09	+0.51
	Transformer-DLCL-25L	27.55	+0.97
EN→ZH	Transformer-Base	25.54	–
	Transformer-Big	26.59	+1.05
	Transformer-DLCL-25L	27.30	+1.76

3   System

3.1   Architecture

The model architecture of the whole system is presented in Fig. 1. It consists of two parts: a predictor which joint left-to-right and right-to-left Pre-norm Transformer-DLCL, and an estimator with a multi-layer Bi-GRU. Predictor is used to extract semantic information from given machine translation results, according to source-side sentences. In order to fully consider the forward and backward information in the sentences, we use the left-to-right and right-to-left translation models to extract the bidirectional semantic information independently, and then fuse them to obtain the quality vectors. After that, the quality vector is fed into the bidirectional GRU to predict the HTER score or OK/BAD labels. We first pre-train forward and backward translation models, then jointly train the estimator with the predictor to maximize the evaluation capability of the system.

3.1.1   Deep Bi-Predictor

The sequence-to-sequence based Transformer models [16] are powerful in extracting information and have been proven to be strong in many translation tasks. The Pre-Norm Transformer-DLCL further improves the feature extraction ability. The encoder receives the input sequence $x = \{x_0, x_1...x_n\}$, and maps it to a vector $z = \{z_0, z_1...z_n\}$ of the same length, which contains the source sentence feature. The decoder inputs the translation sequence $y = \{y_0, y_1...y_m\}$ and generates a top-level representation containing sufficient semantic and grammatical information.

Due to the existence of the decoder mask, the unidirectional model can not observe the future information. In order to make the vector extracted by the model contain sufficient context knowledge, we use left-to-right and right-to-left translation models respectively, and extract the feature vectors $l2r$ and $r2l$ independently. We get the final quality vector by concatenating way ($q = [l2r : r2l]$).

3.1.2 Bi-GRU Estimator

RNN is widely used to solve sequence generation problem. And we use a Bi-GRU as our estimator. The Bi-GRU consists of two parts, forward and backward. It reads quality vector q, calculate the forward hidden states $(\overrightarrow{\mathbf{h}}_1, \cdots, \overrightarrow{\mathbf{h}}_T)$ and backward hidden states $(\overleftarrow{\mathbf{h}}_1, \cdots, \overleftarrow{\mathbf{h}}_T)$ respectively, where T is the sequence length. We get the representation of each word by concatenating the forward hidden state $\overrightarrow{\mathbf{h}}_j$ and the backward one $\overleftarrow{\mathbf{h}}_j$, $h_j = [\overrightarrow{\mathbf{h}}_j, \overleftarrow{\mathbf{h}}_j]$. We convert the word-level tasks into classification problems, and Eqs. 2 and 3 show our goals on the word and gap tasks, respectively. Sentence-level tasks are converted to a regression problem, refer to Eq. 4.

$$\arg\min \sum_{j=1}^{T} \mathbf{cross\_entropy}\,(y_j, \mathbf{W}_1 h_j) \tag{2}$$

$$\arg\min \sum_{j=0}^{T} \mathbf{cross\_entropy}\,(y_j, \mathbf{W}_2 \mathbf{Conv}(h_j, h_{j+1})) \tag{3}$$

$$\arg\min \|h - \mathbf{sigmoid}\,(\mathbf{W}_3 \mathbf{h}_T)\|_2^2 \tag{4}$$

where h is the real HTER score, y_j is real labels, $\mathbf{W}_1$, $\mathbf{W}_2$ and $\mathbf{W}_3$ is trainable parameter matrices, and T is the length of the target-side. **cross_entropy** is the cross entropy loss (with logits). **Conv** is a convolution operation that fuses information from adjacent locations for predicting gap tags.

We dynamically control the number of layers of the Bi-GRU according to different data volumes. At the same time, we also try the self-attention layer and self-attention layer + Bi-GRU architectures as estimator, finding there is no better performance. But we use them as candidate models for ensemble to enhance diversity.

3.1.3 BPE Matrix

BPE is introduced to reduce the number of unknown tokens in many NLP tasks. And we also apply it to our model. But there is a problem in word-level task. The length L_b of quality vector extracted by predictor is different from the number L_w of tokens in sentence. We follow Fan et al. [5] to solve this problem by a $L_w \times L_b$ sparse matrix, which average the features of subwords corresponding to one word token, and reduce the length of quality vector from L_b to L_w.

3.2 Data Construction

3.2.1 Bilingual Data for Pre-training

We use WMT 2019 ZH-EN parallel data to pre-train our predictors, which consists of CWMT, wikititles-v1, NewsCommentary-v14 and UN corpus. After filtering, about 11M sentences pair is selected. Furthermore, we use 6M monolingual data from WMT 2019 to construct pseudo data by back-translation [3] in both directions. All parallel data is segmented by NiuTrans [18] word segmentation toolkit. After the preprocessing, we train BPE [12] models with 32, 000 merge operations for both sides respectively.

3.2.2 Quality Estimation Data

The dataset for QE task consists of three parts: source sentences, machine translations and QEscore (HTER score for sentence level or OK/BAD labels for word-level). The amount of data provided by CCMT 2019 QE task is no more than 15K. We think it isn't enough to train a strong model, so we construct 50K pseudo data using parallel data from WMT 2019. To obtain high quality bilingual data, we use machine translation model and language model to score parallel data. First, we use the translation model to score the real bilingual data by forced decoding. Secondly, we use the language model to score the source and target sentences, and combine the three scores to sort the real data, select the data with the higher score. After obtaining high-quality bilingual data, we decode them in a variety of ways to obtain machine-translated data, including beam search [11], sampling-topk. We regard the target sentences of bilingual data as personal edited data, and generate the sentence-level HTER score or the word-level labels using TER tool [14].

In addition, we find the ratio of OK/BAD labels in word gap subtask is about 20:1, which means the BAD labels between words corresponding to missing translations is too few and it's hard to predict BAD label for trained model. So we randomly drop some word in our machine translation results to improve the number of BAD label between words.

3.3 Model Ensemble

In MT systems, ensemble decoding method is wildly used to boost translation quality via integrating the predictions of several single models at each decode step. We try a similar approach in QE task. However, we find that ensemble method is expensive when it comes to more model fusion. It can't try to combine more models in a limited time, so we adopt an external fusion method:

- We select twelve high-scoring single models using different model architectures or datasets, and decode 12 results as candidates.
- Calculate all combinations of twelve models externally.
- For different combinations, word-level tasks, we use the voting method to ensemble, and the sentence-level we average HTER score.
- Pick the best performing model combination.

In this way, we quickly try out all the combinations of candidates in a short time, and it is easier to pick the optimal combination.

4 Experiments and Results

We implement our QE models based on Fairseq [10]. Transformer-DLCL models are pre-trained on eight 1080Ti GPUs. We use the Adam optimizer with $\beta_1 = 0.97$, $\beta_2 = 0.997$ and $\epsilon = 10^{-6}$. The training data is reshuffled after finishing

Table 2. Word-level word result on CCMT QE *valid2019*. We use a jointly l2r and r2l Transformer-DLCL as a predictor and Bi-GRU as an estimator to jointly train with different datasets.

Construction method	F1-OK	F1-BAD	F1-multi
–	0.8353	0.5673	0.4739
High quality bilingual	0.8642	0.5897	0.5096
Bilingual-beam	0.8735	0.5747	0.502
Bilingual-sampling-topk	0.8691	0.5795	0.5036
Bilingual-round-trip	0.8632	0.5833	0.5035

each training epoch, and we batch sentence pairs by target-side sentences lengths, with 8192 tokens per GPU. Large learning rate and warmup-steps are chosen for faster convergence. We set max learning rate as 0.002 and warmup-steps as 8000. For the jointly training predictor-estimator architecture, we train it on one 1080Ti GPU, 1024 tokens per step. And we set max learning rate as 0.0005 and warmup-steps as 200.

Moreover, due to the lack of BAD labels in the word-level tasks are relatively small, the model tends to predict all labels as OK in the inference stage. So we introduce the bad-enhanced parameter, strengthen the weight of the BAD label when calculating the loss, thereby improving the ability of the model to predict BAD. Next, we will show details in the following subsections.

4.1 QE Pseudo Data

We compare different method on the task of ZH2EN word-level. The following will introduce the method we use.

- Use high-quality bilingual data such as newtest2016, newtest2017, and use the target as the result of personal editing, and decode the source to construct dataset by sampling-topk.
- The data selected from the bilingual data, and the pseudo datasets decoded by the beam search [11] or the Sampling-topk.
- We translate the monolingual data in target side to the source sentences, and then translate generated sentences back to target side, this method names round-trip [6]. The detail results are shown in Table 2.

The round-trip and sampling-topk methods are mainly aimed at the unbalanced distribution of OK and BAD labels in word-level tasks. We increase the number of BAD tags by introducing noise during the decoding process. The Table 2 shows that pseudo-data using high-quality bilingual constructs delivers the greatest performance improvement in the same architecture. However, there are no significant differences in the average label distribution in the results by introducing noise in a variety of ways. We speculate that the target language in

Table 3. Word-level result on CCMT QE *valid2019*. We use GRU as an estimator to jointly train using officially available data.

Task	Precitor	F1-OK	F1-BAD	F1-multi
ZH2EN word-level word	Transformer-base	0.8932	0.4618	0.4125
	Transformer-Big	0.8946	0.4709	0.4212
	Deep Transformer-DLCL	0.8477	0.5078	0.4305
ZH2EN word-level gap	Transformer-base	0.9511	0.1682	0.1600
	Transformer-Big	0.9516	0.1976	0.1881
	Deep Transformer-DLCL	0.9552	0.1981	0.1892
EN2ZH word-level word	Transformer-base	0.8896	0.4043	0.3597
	Transformer-Big	0.8904	0.4176	0.3718
	Deep Transformer-DLCL	0.8727	0.4309	0.3761
EN2ZH word-level gap	Transformer-base	0.9585	0.1454	0.1394
	Transformer-Big	0.9472	0.149	0.1411
	Deep Transformer-DLCL	0.9493	0.1533	0.1455

high-quality bilingual data is closer to the personal editing results, and the generated tags are more consistent with the real data, which makes the model more accurate. Different datasets are also used to increase data diversity in model fusion.

4.2   Different Predictor

Our model base on the predictor-estimator architecture. Recent research shows that the Transformer [16] has powerful information extraction capability. Therefore, we use the translation model as a predictor to extract the semantic information contained in the sentence. At the same time, we empirically believe that a stronger translation model can bring greater performance improvement to the QE task. In order to verify the impact of the pre-trained translation model on the QE model, we conduct multiple experiments with different left-to-right predictors and the same estimator. The result of word-level is shown on Table 3, Sentence-level on Table 4.

From the Tables 3 and 4, we find the estimator has better performance with more powerful translation model.

4.3   Different Estimator

After determining the architecture of the predictor, we try a variety of architectures as the estimator, including GRU, Bi-GRU and self-attention. We take the task of the ZH-EN word-level as an example. In Table 5, we show different prediction results in different architectures.

Table 4. Sentence-level result on CCMT QE *valid2019*. We use GRU as an estimator to jointly train using officially available data.

Task	Precitor	Person's
ZH2EN sentence-level	Transformer-base	0.5548
	Transformer-Big	0.5645
	Transformer-DLCL	0.5699
EN2ZH sentence-level	Transformer-base	0.4696
	Transformer-Big	0.4872
	Transformer-DLCL	0.5071

Table 5. ZH2EN word-level word result on CCMT QE *valid2019*. We use a jointly l2r and r2l Transformer-DLCL as a predictor.

Estimator	F1-OK	F1-BAD	F1-multi
GRU	0.8731	0.5427	0.4738
Bi-GRU	0.8642	0.5897	0.5096
Self-attention	0.8165	0.5265	0.4299
Self-attention + Bi-GRU	0.8511	0.5519	0.4697

We use real data and high-quality bilingual constructed pseudo-data total 30k as jointly training data. We can observe that Bi-GRU performs significantly better than other architectures with the same dataset. However, due to the possibility of data scarcity that makes complex architecture trained inadequately, we also try to increase the amount of pseudo-data for the self-attention layer and self-attention + Bi-GRU architecture. We found that increasing the amount of data lead to the performance improvement of more complex estimator architectures. But it's still a little worse than the Bi-GRU. We use them as seed models for system integration to increase diversity.

4.4   Ensemble

We construct multiple sub-models through different model architectures and data sets, and integrate the results of multiple systems externally on all tasks to further improve the stability and performance of the system. We use the left-to-right Transformer-DLCL as the predictor and the GRU as the estimator to build our baseline system. Table 6 shows the final results of all of our participating tasks.

Table 6. All word-level and sentence-level result on CCMT QE *valid2019*.

System	ZH2EN						
	Word-level word			Word-level gap			Sentence-level
	F1-OK	F1-BAD	F1-multi	F1-OK	F1-BAD	F1-multi	Person's
Baseline	0.8477	0.5078	0.4305	0.9552	0.1981	0.1892	0.5699
+Bi-GRU	0.8673	0.5215	0.4523	0.9556	0.2116	0.2022	0.5802
+r2l predictor	0.8353	0.5673	0.4739	0.9570	0.2583	0.2472	0.5831
+Pseudo data	0.8642	0.5897	0.5096	0.9615	0.2776	0.2669	0.5830
+Ensemble	0.8767	0.6152	0.5393	0.9622	0.2887	0.2778	0.6164
System	EN2ZH						
	Word-level word			Word-level gap			Sentence-level
	F1-OK	F1-BAD	F1-multi	F1-OK	F1-BAD	F1-multi	Person's
Baseline	0.8727	0.4309	0.3761	0.9493	0.1533	0.1455	0.5071
+Bi-GRU	0.8932	0.4692	0.4199	0.9671	0.1669	0.1614	0.5501
+r2l predictor	0.898	0.4695	0.4217	0.9596	0.179	0.1718	0.5537
+Pseudo data	0.8941	0.4762	0.4258	0.9656	0.2083	0.2011	0.5491
+Ensemble	0.8974	0.4886	0.4385	0.9715	0.2283	0.2218	0.5861

5 Conclusion

This paper describes our systems for CCMT19 Quality Estimate tasks including both word-level and sentence-level.

We adopt predictor-estimator architecture, use Transformer-DLCL as Predictor based on deep network [1], and combine left-to-right and right-to-left models to further enhance predictor's feature extraction capabilities. Estimator adopts the Bi-GRU and uses the quality vector extracted by predictor to predict for different tasks.

At the same time, we further improve the performance of the translation model as predictor and the prediction performance of estimator by artificially constructing pseudo-data. In addition, a external ensemble algorithm is helpful to search a robust combination of models.

Acknowledgments. This work was supported in part by the National Science Foundation of China (Nos. 61876035, 61732005 and 61432013), the National Key R&D Program of China (No. 2019QY1801) and the Opening Project of Beijing Key Laboratory of Internet Culture and Digital Dissemination Research. We also thank the reviewers for their insightful comments.

References

1. Bapna, A., Chen, M.X., Firat, O., Cao, Y., Wu, Y.: Training deeper neural machine translation models with transparent attention. arXiv preprint arXiv:1808.07561 (2018)
2. Blatz, J., et al.: Confidence estimation for machine translation. In: Coling 2004: Proceedings of the 20th International Conference on Computational Linguistics (2004)
3. Douglas, S.P., Craig, C.S.: Collaborative and iterative translation: an alternative approach to back translation. J. Int. Mark. **15**(1), 30–43 (2007)
4. Edunov, S., Ott, M., Auli, M., Grangier, D.: Understanding back-translation at scale. arXiv preprint arXiv:1808.09381 (2018)
5. Fan, K., Li, B., Zhou, F., Wang, J.: "Bilingual expert" can find translation errors, July 2018
6. Junczys-Dowmunt, M., Grundkiewicz, R.: Log-linear combinations of monolingual and bilingual neural machine translation models for automatic post-editing. In: WMT (2016)
7. Kim, H., Jung, H.Y., Kwon, H., Lee, J.H., Na, S.H.: Predictor-estimator: neural quality estimation based on target word prediction for machine translation. ACM Trans. Asian Low-Resour. Lang. Inf. Process. (TALLIP) **17**(1), 3 (2017)
8. Ba, J.L., Kiros, J.R., Hinton, G.E.: Layer normalization. arXiv preprint arXiv:1607.06450 (2016)
9. Niehues, J., Herrmann, T., Vogel, S., Waibel, A.: Wider context by using bilingual language models in machine translation. In: Proceedings of the Sixth Workshop on Statistical Machine Translation, pp. 198–206. Association for Computational Linguistics (2011)
10. Ott, M., et al.: fairseq: A fast, extensible toolkit for sequence modeling. In: Proceedings of NAACL-HLT 2019: Demonstrations (2019)
11. Sennrich, R., Haddow, B., Birch, A.: Improving neural machine translation models with monolingual data. arXiv preprint arXiv:1511.06709 (2015)
12. Sennrich, R., Haddow, B., Birch, A.: Neural machine translation of rare words with subword units. arXiv preprint arXiv:1508.07909 (2015)
13. Shaw, P., Uszkoreit, J., Vaswani, A.: Self-attention with relative position representations. arXiv preprint arXiv:1803.02155 (2018)
14. Snover, M., Dorr, B., Schwartz, R., Micciulla, L., Makhoul, J.: A study of translation edit rate with targeted human annotation. In: Proceedings of Association for Machine Translation in the Americas, vol. 200 (2006)
15. Specia, L., Paetzold, G., Scarton, C.: Multi-level translation quality prediction with quest++. In: Proceedings of ACL-IJCNLP 2015 System Demonstrations, pp. 115–120 (2015)
16. Vaswani, A., et al.: Attention is all you need. In: Advances in Neural Information Processing Systems, pp. 6000–6010 (2017)
17. Wang, Q., et al.: Learning deep transformer models for machine translation. arXiv preprint arXiv:1906.01787 (2019)
18. Xiao, T., Zhu, J., Zhang, H., Li, Q.: Niutrans: an open source toolkit for phrase-based and syntax-based machine translation. In: Proceedings of the ACL 2012 System Demonstrations ACL 2012, pp. 19–24. Association for Computational Linguistics, Stroudsburg, PA, USA (2012). http://dl.acm.org/citation.cfm?id=2390470.2390474

Tencent Minority-Mandarin Translation System

Bojie Hu[1(✉)], Ambyer Han[1], Zheyang Zhang[2], Shen Huang[1], and Qi Ju[1]

[1] Tencent Minority-Mandarin Translation, Beijing, China
`{bojiehu,ambyera,springhuang,damonju}@tencent.com`
[2] Natural Language Processing Lab, Northeastern University, Shenyang, China
`zhangzheyang1995@outlook.com`

Abstract. This paper describes the submissions of the Tencent minority-mandarin translation system for CCMT19. We participate in 3 translation directions including Uighur→Chinese, Tibetan→Chinese and Mongolian→Chinese. Our systems are neural machine translation systems trained with our improved Marian, and are called TenTrans, which are based on Google's Transformer model architecture. We also adopt most techniques that have been proven effective recently in academia, such as back-translation based sampling, data selection, sequence-level knowledge distillation, ensemble distillation, model ensembling and reranking. By using the above technologies, our submitted systems achieve a stable performance improvement.

Keywords: TenTrans · Back-translation · Knowledge distillation · Ensemble distillation · Reranking

1 Introduction

End-to-end neural machine translation (NMT) [1–5] based on self-attention mechanism [6], the Transformer, has become promising paradigm in field of machine translation academia and industry. This paper describes the submissions of the Tencent minority-mandarin translation system for the 15th China Conference on Machine Translation (CCMT 2019). We participate in the CCMT19 translation tasks in 3 different language pairs: Uighur→Chinese, Tibetan→Chinese and Mongolian→Chinese. The training part of this paper is an improvement on Marian[1][7] NMT whose Transformer architecture part. And the inference part is completely original. And we call our systems TenTrans [8].

Our experimental setup is based on recent promising techniques in NMT, many of which have also been applied to submitted system [9] last year, including Byte Pair Encoding (BPE) [10] to achieve open-vocabulary translation [11],

---

[1] https://github.com/marian-nmt/marian.

B. Hu, A. Han, Z. Zhang—Equal contribution.

S. Huang and K. Knight (Eds.): CCMT 2019, CCIS 1104, pp. 93–104, 2019.
https://doi.org/10.1007/978-981-15-1721-1_10

back-translation [12] to make use of extra monolingual data to augment training data and multi-model fusion techniques. In addition to the above techniques, as for data augmentation, several different back-translation methods are experimented, including methods based on pure beam search, unrestricted sampling and restricted sampling (top-k) proposed by [13,14]. And we propose a simpler alternative to noising techniques, consisting of tagging back-translated source sentences with an extra token. Furthermore, iterative back-translation [15], a method for generating increasingly better synthetic parallel data from monolingual data, is tried.

With regard to model fine-tuning, sequence-level knowledge distillation [16] and ensemble distillation [17] methods are adopted. Model diversity is a key component in building strong NMT ensembles [18,19]. Therefore, all the models we use for ensembling are trained from scratch and did not use the pre-trained model for warm starting. Moreover, more diverse methods are used to generate every single model, for example, different initialization methods, model sizes, model architecture and dropout [20] parameters, etc. In addition, we adopt the K-batched MIRA algorithm [21] to rerank the n-best list.

The paper is structured as follows: Sect. 2 describes the novelties of our model architecture compared to standard Transformer implementation (tensor2tensor[2]), then we present the technologies used in TenTrans in detail in Sect. 3. Section 4 describes our experimental settings and results, and Sect. 5 concludes the paper.

2 Model Features

In this work, the forward translator is trained on our improved Marian NMT [7], and back-translator is trained on Fairseq[3] [22]. The latter is used to generate synthetic source sentences by unrestricted sampling and restricted top-k sampling. Two network structures are adopted, Transformer base model (embedding size 512, feed-forward layers with inner dimension 2048, 8 attention heads) and Transformer big model[4] (embedding size 1024, feed-forward with inner dimension 4096, 8 attention heads, transformer-dropout, transformer-dropout-attention, transformer-dropout-ffn are all set to 0.1).

Minimum likelihood estimation (MLE) as loss function is applied to train all the models using Adam [23] ($\beta_1 = 0.9$, $\beta_2 = 0.98$, $\epsilon = 10^{-9}$). We use synchronous training and data parallelism on 8 NVIDIA Tesla P40 GPUs. Learning rate is increased linearly for first 16000 updates and decreased at $16000/sqrt(up.)$, where $up.$ means number of updates. The gradient norm [24] is clipped to 5.0 and label smoothing [25] is applied with $\epsilon_{ls} = 0.1$. Swish proposed by [26] is used as our Transformer model's activation function. We early stop training [19] when there is no new maximum value of the validation BLEU [27] for 10 consecutive

---

[2] https://github.com/tensorflow/tensor2tensor.

[3] https://github.com/pytorch/fairseq.

[4] This setting is slightly different from big model in tensor2tensor and Fairseq, which is the best parameter setting we have ever tried.

save-points (saving every 2000 updates) and select the model with the highest BLEU score on the validation set. Contrary to [6] or [19], we do not average checkpoints, but maintain a continuously updated exponentially averaged model over the entire training.

Data weighting [28–30] is commonly used as a domain adaptation technique, which weights each data item according to its proximity to the in-domain data. Our improved Marain NMT supports sentence weighting strategies. Compared with [28,29], we propose a novel sentence weighting method for domain adaptation of neural machine translation. The similarity of each sentence to the target domain is calculated by a binary classifier. The binary classifier consists of BERT [31] pre-trained model and a two-layer feedforward network. We discuss the specific approach in detail in Sect. 3.2.

In addition, TenTrans can handle custom embedding vectors trained with word2vec[5] or other tools. Moreover, guided alignment training [32] is also supported by TenTrans, which is only needed to provide a word alignment file trained with *fast align* toolkit[6] or other alignment tools. To alleviate poor translation performance of named entities, we follow NER generalization method used in [8].

3 Experimental Techniques

In this section, experimental techniques used in our submitted systems will be introduced.

3.1 Data Enhancement

For low-resource languages, the use of additional monolingual corpus[7] is crucial as the target side lexicon coverage is often insufficient, especially our participated language pairs only consist of 0.16~0.26M bilingual data. An effective method to use monolingual data is to augment the parallel training corpus with back-translations [12] of target language sentences. 6.5M monolingual sentences are remained after a series of data cleaning processes. We use data selection methods described in Sect. 3.2 to select in-domain sentences from them. From Table 1 we can see that the binary classification method do not show stronger performance than N-grams method. Here, we mainly use N-grams method to select data. But we use binary classification method in Sect. 3.3, and we've shown a lot of performance improvements there. Then comes the question of how many back translated data should be used. The data quantity experimental results in Table 1 show that it's difficult to have an universal recipe for all languages. For example, with increasing the amount of used monolingual data on Uighur→Chinese and Tibetan→Chinese tasks, the performance of back-translation is on the rise. But when used monolingual data on Mongolian→Chinese tasks are increased from

---

[5] https://code.google.com/archive/p/word2vec/.
[6] https://github.com/clab/fast_align.
[7] *XMU* corpus: http://nlp.nju.edu.cn/cwmt2018/resources.html.

Table 1. Data enhancement experiment. BT. means back-translation. Uighur →Chinese (UY2ZH) uses the Transformer base model for comparative experiments, and the other two languages use Transformer big model. The comparative experimental settings in each language pairs are different, so some of the experimental results are not listed in the table. In the data quantity experiment, all systems adopt back-translation method based on beam search. In the data quality experiment, Uighur→Chinese and Mongolian→Chinese (MN2ZH) systems are carried on the contrast experiment on 3M sentences, and the other is on 5M sentences. In the data domain experiment, UY2ZH system is carried on the contrast experiment on 1M sentences, and Tibetan→Chinese (TI2ZH) system is on 3M sentences. And MN2ZH system adopts N-grams method by default. The corresponding settings highlighted in boldface in the table are the experimental settings used by our final submitted systems. The experimental settings and scoring method are described in detail in Sect. 4.

Data quantity experiment			
Monolingual data quantity (sents.)	UY2ZH (Base)	TI2ZH (Big)	MN2ZH (Big)
1M	29.25	–	64.49
2M	29.88	–	–
3M	**29.91**	23.13	**63.84**
5M	–	**23.54**	–
6.5M	29.78	–	58.93
Data quality experiment			
BT. methods	UY2ZH (Base)	TI2ZH (Big)	MN2ZH (Big)
Baseline	22.38	20.94	62.69
Beam search [12]	29.91	**23.54**	**63.84**
Sampling [13]	29.79	16.24	58.76
Top-k sampling [13]	29.87	17.03	63.97
Iterative BT. [15]	29.82	–	–
Tagged BT.	**30.21**	–	–
Data domain experiment			
Data selection methods	UY2ZH (1M)	TI2ZH (3M)	MN2ZH (3M)
Random	28.99	22.71	–
N-grams (Sect. 3.2)	**29.25**	**23.13**	**63.84**
Binary classification (Sect. 3.2)	29.14	–	–

1M sentences to 6.5M sentences, the performance degradation is very obvious. The main reason of this phenomenon is the domain of the monolingual data is different from the train and validation set. The monolingual data belongs to news domain, while the fields of train and validation set is complicated, including spoken language, news, laws and regulations.

In order to investigate the effect of the quality of synthetic data on back-translation method, we adopt the unrestricted sampling and top-k sampling methods proposed by [13]. Both these two methods introduce more uncertainty and noise to the synthetic, but [13] points out that synthetic data based on sampling or noised beam search provides a stronger training signal than synthetic data based on argmax inference [12]. In addition, we tried iterative back-translation [15], a method for generating increasingly better synthetic data. Data quality experimental results in Table 1 show that none of these methods can significantly improve the performance than beam search based back-translation method in low-resource scenarios. What's more, we propose a novel approach, we call Tagged Back-translation, which can indicate to model whether a given training sentence is back-translated or genuine bi-text. We tag our synthetic training data by prepending a reserved token to the input sequence, which is then treated in the same way as any other tokens. Experimental results (Tagged BT.) in Table 1 show that the method is simple and effective. We suspect that in the case of very few genuine bi-texts, this indication information is important for model training.

3.2 Data Selection Methods

Previous work [33,34] has verified the importance of data quality and data domain in building a machine translation system. As for data quality aspect, we firstly filter out bilingual sentences with unrecognizable code, large length ratio difference, duplications and wrong language coding, then filter out bi-texts with poor mutual translation rate by using *fast-align* toolkit. The cleaning process of monolingual corpus is similar to that of the previous one. In this section, we focus on how to use data selection methods to select sentences that are closer to the target domain. In our work, we try two different approaches to select in-domain corpus, namely, n-grams and binary classification. The latter is our original method.

N-Grams: We exploit the method proposed in [35], which aims at selecting in-domain sentence pairs from general domain corpus by in-domain language model. In our experiment, the Chinese side of bi-texts and monolingual corpus are regarded as general domain corpus G, while the Chinese side of development sets and test sets of previous years about 6.5K are regarded as in-domain corpus I. We firstly train tri-gram language models over I, namely LM_I. Then, build tri-gram language models of similar size over the random sample from G, namely LM_G. Based on this, the score of each sentence s in G is computed as $|LM_I^s - LM_G^s|$. The lower the score, the closer the sentence is to the target domain, and vice versa.

Binary Classification: Although there are only 6.5K sentences in-domain data, we have 6.5M sentences unlabeled monolingual data from general domain. To exploit large amounts of unlabeled data, we adopt a semi-supervised learning framework similar to [28,36]. [36] first learns word embedding from unlabeled monolingual data using *word2vec* [37], then generates continuous representation for every unlabeled sentence. Based on the trained word embedding, the in-domain data as positive sample and randomly sampled general-domain data as negative sample are combined to train domain classifier with semi-supervised

CNN, then domain relevance scores for every sentence in G are calculated by this domain classifier.

Compared with [28,36], we do not use *word2vec* to learn the representation model, but use the BERT[8] [31] which has the stronger representation ability to learn. What's more, we then pass sentence representation vector x calculated on pre-trained BERT model into a two-layer feedforward network instead of CNN. To get a probability value between 0 and 1, we use softmax as this two-layer feedforward network's activation function. The domain similarity probability P_{ds} of a sentence x is computed as follows.

$$P_{ds}(x) = \text{softmax}\left(\tanh\left(W_1 x + b_1\right)^T W_2 + b_2\right) \tag{1}$$

where W_1, W_2, b_1, b_2 are trainable parameters.

We extract 1K sentences from positive sample set as development set, and remove the 1K sentences from positive sample set. We train this binary classifier with a cross-entropy loss, maximizing $P_{ds}(x)$ for sentences drawn from positive sample set, and minimizing it for those drawn from negative sample set. We early stop training when there is no new minimum value of the validation loss for 3 consecutive validation (one validation per epoch on the development set). Since we randomly select sentences from the G as negative sample, the selected sentences domain are likely to be very close to in-domain. Therefore, we re-score the sentences in G with this binary classification model and select the sentences closest to 0 as the negative samples of the new round of training. The number of selected sentences is about the same as that of I. We retrain the binary classification model with new negative samples and the original positive samples. And the process iterates until the classification accuracy is no longer increased on the development set. Then comes the question of what if new negative sample after each round of training is still very close to I. In the course of our experiment, there is a very large gap between new negative sample and sentences in I.

3.3   Data Weighting

We measure the similarity between sentences in general domain G and the in-domain I using the binary classification method mentioned in Sect. 3.2. The similarity is used to scale our costs to emphasize training sentences that are similar to our development set. Therefore, we use the following objective function:

$$\theta' = \arg\max_\theta \sum_{(x,y)\in D} (1 + p_{ds}(x)) \log p(y|x; \theta) \tag{2}$$

We apply a cost weighting method by adding 1 to the normalized probability [28]. This is to give the origin training data a bonus to some degree. In addition, the languages pairs we participate in are all low-resource. That is, we need to use back-translation methods to generate synthetic sentences, then training corpora

---

[8] The used BERT is developed by our department's NLP team.

is constructed with genuine bi-texts and synthetic sentences. Therefore, the p_{ds} values of all sentences in genuine bi-texts are always equal to 1, while the P_{ds} values of all sentences in synthetic data are calculated according to Formula 1.

3.4   Fine-Tune with Knowledge Distillation Methods

For low resource scenarios, we find that the fine-tuning method proposed by [38] is very effective, which continues to train the already trained back-translation system on the genuine parallel corpus. In addition, the two knowledge distillation methods proposed by [16], KD and Inter, are also used to continue to fine-tuning our single model. We retranslate the full training corpus source data with teacher model to generate the translations with the highest model score. Next, we train our student models exclusively on the newly generated output. [16] refers to this method as KD. The Inter method refers to not choosing the translation with the highest model score, but choosing the translation with the highest sentence-level BLEU score with regard to the origin target corpus. What's more, we use ensemble distillation approach proposed by [17] to transfer the translation quality of an ensemble teacher network into a single NMT system.

3.5   Reranking

We apply the reranking module to pick up a better hypothesis from the n-best generated by ensemble decoding. Our reranking features include:

Right to Left (R2L) Models: There is a tendency for the prefix part of translation candidates to be higher quality than the suffix part in the current translation models [39]. In order to alleviate this problem, we train 3 R2L models based on Transformer big model architecture, each of which is the best model after fine-tuning model with genuine bi-texts. The experimental results show that this feature is very strong and plays a vital role in reranking.

Target to Source (T2S) Models: Neural machine translation models often have the phenomena of missing translation, repeated translation, and obvious translation deviation [40]. To alleviate this problem, we train 4 T2S models, which are also based on Transformer big model.

Language Models (LMs): We use 5-gram language models trained on $KenLM^9$ and Transformer language models trained on Marian.

Word Penalty (WP): From the translation results of the development set, we can see that the length of some candidates is quite different from that of the reference translation, so we use the feature widely used in statistical machine translation, word penalty feature. This feature is relatively simple, that is, the length of each candidate.

We adopt K-batched MIRA algorithm [21] to rerank the n-best list.

---

[9] https://github.com/kpu/kenlm.

Table 2. BLEU scores [%] on development sets for our submitted Uighur→Chinese, Tibetan→Chinese and Mongolian→Chinese systems. * denotes the submitted system.

System	UY2ZH	TI2ZH	MN2ZH
Transformer base model	22.38	19.99	61.39
+BT. beam search [12]	29.91(+7.53)	–	61.54(+0.15)
+Guided alignment [32]	29.78(+7.4)	–	62.44(+1.05)
+Data weighting	31.39(+9.01)	–	60.60(−0.79)
Transformer big model	24.36	20.94	62.69
+BT. beam search [12]	31.56(+7.2)	23.54(+2.60)	63.84(+1.15)
+Tagged BT.	31.64(+7.28)	–	–
+Data weighting	32.14(+7.78)	23.8(+2.86)	–
+Fine-tune with Bi-texts [38]	33.05(+8.69)	25.98(+5.04)	67.42(+4.63)
+Fine-tune with KD [16]	33.12(+8.76)	25.81(+4.87)	67.15(+4.46)
+Fine-tune with inter [16]	33.36(+9.0)	–	66.43(+3.74)
+Fine-tune with ensemble KD [17]	34.22(+9.86)	–	–
+Ensemble	34.51(+10.15)	27.77(+6.83)	70.23(+7.54)
+Reranking*	**35.54(+11.18)**	**28.69(+7.75)**	**70.65(+7.96)**

4 Experiments and Results

We report the experimental results of Uighur→Chinese and Mongolian→Chinese system on official development set, and the experimental results of Tibetan→ Chinese system on the development set extracted by ourselves. Because we find that Tibetan→Chinese translation task official development set is very short and of poor quality, with an average sentence length of only 7.2 words and mostly phrases rather than sentences. Therefore, we extracted 1000 sentences from the 0.15M sentences high-quality bilingual data to use as the new development set, with the average sentence length is 20.2 words, which is filtered out of the bilingual data. Token-based BLEU-4 scores are reported by *multi-bleu.pl* in UY2ZH and TI2ZH, and character-based BLEU-4 scores are reported by *mteval-v13a.pl* in MN2ZH.

In all our participated tasks, the Chinese sentences are segmented using *scws* toolkit[10]. For Uighur, Tibetan, and Mongolian sentences, we use our original tokenizer. Data cleaning processes can be seen in Sect. 3.2. After data cleaning, the bilingual corpus of Uighur→Chinese, Tibetan→Chinese and Mongolian→ Chinese left 0.16M, 0.15M, 0.24M sentence pairs, respectively. In final submitted systems, 3M monolingual sentences selected by N-grams data selection approach are used in Uighur→Chinese and Mongolian→Chinese tasks, and 5M sentences are used in Tibetan→Chinese task. We train BPE [10] models with 32 K merge operations for both sides respectively in Uighur→Chinese and Tibetan→Chinese

---

[10] http://www.xunsearch.com/scws/.

tasks, 16K merge operations for both sides respectively in Mongolian→Chinese tasks. All tasks beam size of decoding are set to 24. The length penalty α of decoding in UY2ZH, TI2ZH, and MN2ZH tasks are set to 1.5, 1.2, 1.2 respectively. In addition, we use post-process scripts to remove some clearly duplicate translation.

Transformer base model is mainly used for comparative experiments, and our final systems are trained based on Transformer big model. From Table 2, we can see that back-translation is strong in a low-resource scenario, especially increasing 7.2 BLEU value in Uighur→Chinese tasks. The reason for the less obvious promotion in Mongolian→Chinese tasks is the domain problem of monolingual corpus. Guided alignment training does not show significant gains in low-resource scenario and is not adopted by our final systems. Data weighting based on our proposed binary classification method shows consistent performance improvements over Uighur→Chinese and Tibetan→Chinese tasks. We analyze that this method can not only solve the domain adaptation problem, but also to some extent alleviate the problem of diluting the few genuine bi-texts in a large number of synthetic data in low-resource scenario.

As for fine-tuning, using bi-texts to fine-tune the trained back-translation model method is very effective, which brings obvious gains to all tasks. Using KD and Inter method to fine-tune system, it brings a slight improvement of 0.31 BLEU values on Uighur→Chinese task, but decreasing on the other tasks. On Uighur→Chinese task, we use ensemble distillation method to transfer 4 teacher models into a single student model. It improves the performance of a single model by 0.86 BLEU values. However, the performance improvement is not very obvious when ensemble multiple models. In contrast, the other two tasks that did not use this method improved significantly when ensemble multiple models. Last but not least, reranking n-best method still shows obvious effectiveness.

We submitted Uighur→Chinese system is 4.26 BLEU[11] values higher than the best system last year when the data is significantly less than last year. Our submitted Mongolian→Chinese and Tibetan→Chinese systems are 8.13 BLEU values and 2 BLEU values higher than the second system last year, respectively.

5   Conclusion

This paper describes Tencent Minority-Mandarin translation system for CCMT19. It mainly focuses on data enhancement, data selection, model fine tuning, model distillation and reranking. The experimental results show that how to use the data correctly is still the most important process of building a strong machine translation system. In particular, the original binary classifier using BERT pre-trained model and a two-layer feedforward network proposed by us is proved to be very effective. In addition, model fine-tuning can not be ignored in the low-resource scenario.

---

[11] Using official scoring programs and requirements.

References

1. Cho, K., Merrienboer, B., Gulcehre, C., Bougares, F., Schwenk, H., Bengio, Y.: Learning phrase representations using RNN encoder-decoder for statistical machine translation. In: EMNLP (2014)
2. Sutskever, I., Vinyals, O., Le, Q.V.: Sequence to sequence learning with neural networks. In: Advances in Neural Information Processing Systems, pp. 3104–3112 (2014)
3. Bahdanau, D., Cho, K., Bengio, Y.: Neural machine translation by jointly learning to align and translate. In: Proceedings of ICLR (2014)
4. Sennrich, R., Haddow, B., Birch, A.: Edinburgh neural machine translation systems for WMT 2016. In: Proceedings of the First Conference on Machine Translation. Association for Computational Linguistics, Berlin, Germany (2016)
5. Wu, Y., et al.: Google's Neural Machine Translation System: Bridging the Gap between Human and Machine Translation. CoRR, abs/1609.08144 (2016)
6. Vaswani, A., et al.: Attention is all you need. In: Advances in Neural Information Processing Systems, pp. 5998–6008 (2017)
7. Junczys-Dowmunt, M., et al.: Marian: fast neural machine translation in C++. In: Proceedings of ACL: System Demonstrations, p. 2018. Association for Computational Linguistics, Melbourne, Australia (2018)
8. Hu, B., Han, A., Huang, S.: TencentFmRD neural machine translation for WMT 2018. In: Proceedings of the Third Conference on Machine Translation: Shared Task Papers. Association for Computational Linguistics, Belgium, Brussels (2018)
9. Hu, B., Han, A., Huang, S.: TencentFmRD neural machine translation system. In: Chen, J., Zhang, J. (eds.) CWMT 2018. CCIS, vol. 954, pp. 111–123. Springer, Singapore (2019). https://doi.org/10.1007/978-981-13-3083-4_11
10. Sennrich, R., Haddow, B., Birch, A.: Neural machine translation of rare words with subword units. In: Proceedings of ACL (2016)
11. Luong, M., Manning, C.D.: Achieving open vocabulary neural machine translation with hybrid word-character models. In: Proceedings of ACL (2016)
12. Sennrich, R., Haddow, B., Birch, A.: Improving neural machine translation models with monolingual data. In: Proceedings of ACL (2016)
13. Edunov, S., Ott, M., Auli, M., Grangier, D.: Understanding back-translation at scale. In: Proceedings of the: Conference on Empirical Methods in Natural Language Processing, p. 2018. Association for Computational Linguistics, Brussels, Belgium (2018)
14. Imamura, K., Fujita, A., Sumita, E.: Enhancement of encoder and attention using target monolingual corpora in neural machine translation. In: Proceedings of the 2nd Workshop on Neural Machine Translation and Generation, pp. 55–63 (2018)
15. Hoang, V.C.D., Koehn, P., Haffari, G., Cohn, T.: Iterative back-translation for neural machine translation. In: Proceedings of the 2nd Workshop on Neural Machine Translation and Generation, pp. 18–24 (2018)
16. Kim, Y., Rush, A.M.: Sequence-level knowledge distillation. In: Proceedings of the 2016 Conference on Empirical Methods in Natural Language Processing, pp. 1317–1327. Association for Computational Linguistics, Austin, Texas (2016)
17. Freitag, M., Al-Onaizan, Y., Sankaran, B.: Ensemble distillation for neural machine translation. arXiv preprint arXiv:1702.01802 (2017)
18. Denkowski, M., Neubig, G.: Stronger baselines for trustable results in neural machine translation. In: Proceedings of the First Workshop on Neural Machine Translation, pp. 18–27 (2017)

19. Sennrich, R., et al.: The University of Edinburgh neural MT systems for WMT 2017. In: Proceedings of the Second Conference on Machine Translation, pp. 389–399 (2017)
20. Srivastava, N., Hinton, G., Krizhevsky, A., Sutskever, I., Salakhutdinov, R.: Dropout: a simple way to prevent neural networks from overfitting. J. Mach. Learn. Res. **15**(1), 1929–1958 (2014)
21. Cherry, C., Foster, G.: Batch tuning strategies for statistical machine translation. In: Proceedings of the 2012 Conference of the North American Chapter of the Association for Computational Linguistics: Human Language Technologies, pp. 427–436. Association for Computational Linguistics (2012)
22. Ott, M., et al.: FAIRSEQ: a fast, extensible toolkit for sequence modeling. In: NAACL HLT 2019 (2019)
23. Kingma, D.P., Ba, J.: Adam: A method for stochastic optimization. arXiv preprint arXiv:1412.6980 (2014)
24. Pascanu, R., Mikolov, T., Bengio, Y.: On the difficulty of training recurrent neural networks. In: International Conference on Machine Learning, pp. 1310–1318 (2013)
25. Szegedy, C., Vanhoucke, V., Ioffe, S., Shlens, J., Wojna, Z.: Rethinking the inception architecture for computer vision. In: Proceedings of the IEEE Conference on Computer Vision and Pattern Recognition, pp. 2818–2826 (2016)
26. Ramachandran, P., Zoph, B., Le, Q.V.: Searching for activation functions. arXiv preprint arXiv:1710.05941 (2017)
27. Papineni, K., Roukos, S., Ward, T., Zhu, W.J.: BLEU: a method for automatic evaluation of machine translation. In: Proceedings of the 40th Annual Meeting on Association for Computational Linguistics, pp. 311–318. Association for Computational Linguistics (2002)
28. Chen, B., Cherry, C., Foster, G., Larkin, S.: Cost weighting for neural machine translation domain adaptation. In: Proceedings of the First Workshop on Neural Machine Translation, pp. 40–46 (2017)
29. Zhang, S., Xiong, D.: Sentence weighting for neural machine translation domain adaptation. In: Proceedings of the 27th International Conference on Computational Linguistics, pp. 3181–3190 (2018)
30. Wang, R., Utiyama, M., Liu, L., Chen, K., Sumita, E.: Instance weighting for neural machine translation domain adaptation. In: Proceedings of the 2017 Conference on Empirical Methods in Natural Language Processing, pp. 1482–1488 (2017)
31. Devlin, J., Chang, M.W., Lee, K., Toutanova, K.: Bert: Pre-training of deep bidirectional transformers for language understanding. arXiv preprint arXiv:1810.04805 (2018)
32. Chen, W., Matusov, E., Khadivi, S., Peter, J.T.: Guided alignment training for topic-aware neural machine translation. arXiv preprint arXiv:1607.01628 (2016)
33. Deng, Y., et al.: Alibaba's neural machine translation systems for WMT 2018. In: Proceedings of the Third Conference on Machine Translation: Shared Task Papers, pp. 368–376 (2018)
34. Junczys-Dowmunt, M.: Microsoft's submission to the WMT 2018 news translation task: how i learned to stop worrying and love the data. In: Proceedings of the Third Conference on Machine Translation: Shared Task Papers, pp. 425–430 (2018)
35. Axelrod, A., He, X., Gao, J.: Domain adaptation via pseudo in-domain data selection. In: Proceedings of the Conference on Empirical Methods in Natural Language Processing, pp. 355–362. Association for Computational Linguistics (2011)
36. Chen, B., Huang, F.: Semi-supervised convolutional networks for translation adaptation with tiny amount of in-domain data. In: Proceedings of The 20th SIGNLL Conference on Computational Natural Language Learning, pp. 314–323 (2016)

37. Mikolov, T., Chen, K., Corrado, G., Dean, J.: Efficient estimation of word representations in vector space. arXiv preprint arXiv:1301.3781 (2013)
38. Luong, M.T., Manning, C.D.: Stanford neural machine translation systems for spoken language domains. In: Proceedings of the International Workshop on Spoken Language Translation, pp. 76–79 (2015)
39. Liu, L., Utiyama, M., Finch, A., Sumita, E.: Agreement on target-bidirectional neural machine translation. In: Proceedings of the 2016 Conference of the North American Chapter of the Association for Computational Linguistics: Human Language Technologies, pp. 411–416 (2016)
40. Tu, Z., Liu, Y., Shang, L., Liu, X., Li, H.: Neural machine translation with reconstruction. In: Thirty-First AAAI Conference on Artificial Intelligence (2017)

CCMT 2019 Machine Translation Evaluation Report

Muyun Yang[1]([✉]), Xixin Hu[1], Hao Xiong[2], Jiayi Wang[3],
Yiliyaer Jiaermuhamaiti[4], Zhongjun He[2], Weihua Luo[3],
and Shujian Huang[4]

[1] School of Computer Science and Technology, Harbin Institute of Technology,
Harbin, China
yangmuyun@hit.edu.cn, xixinhu97@foxmail.com
[2] Baidu Inc., Beijing, China
{xionghao05, hezhongjun}@baidu.com
[3] Alibaba Group Inc., Hangzhou, China
{joanne.wjy, weihua.luowh}@alibaba-inc.com
[4] Department of Computer Science and Technology, Nanjing University,
Nanjing, China
{yilye, huangsj}@nju.edu.cn

Abstract. This paper introduces the evaluation procedure, evaluation data, participants and evaluation results of 2019 (15th) China Conference on Machine Translation (CCMT 2019) evaluation campaign. Compared with the last evaluation campaign (CWMT 2018), CCMT 2019 MT evaluation is characterized as follows: a new speech translation task is fulfilled; the translation quality estimation task is augmented with a word level track in addition to the sentence level track. Meanwhile, CCMT 2019 receives increases in the number of participants and systems submitted. This paper presents the anonymous evaluation results of all tasks, with a brief summarization of the techniques applied in this evaluation campaign.

Keywords: CCMT · Machine translation · Evaluation · Speech translation · Quality estimation

1 Introduction

To promote the research and development of machine translation in China, the China Conference on Machine Translation (CCMT 2019), which is hosted by Chinese Information Processing Society of China (CIPSC), organized an evaluation campaign on machine translation (referred to as CCMT 2019 machine translation evaluation). Following the last evaluation (CWMT 2018), CCMT 2019 machine translation evaluation is featured by the following practices:

- A new task of speech translation in Chinese-English translation direction is augmented, jointly organized with Baidu;
- The quality estimation task is extended, under the support of Alibaba, to word-level quality estimation sub-task, in addition to the existing sentence-level sub-task;

S. Huang and K. Knight (Eds.): CCMT 2019, CCIS 1104, pp. 105–128, 2019.
https://doi.org/10.1007/978-981-15-1721-1_11

- Joint task with WMT 2019 on the evaluation of Chinese-English and English-Chinese translation is continued, with a focus on sharing training corpus;
- The evaluation tasks of Mongolian-Chinese, Tibetan-Chinese, and Uyghur-Chinese translations are reserved, as well as the Japanese-Chinese-English multilingual translation tasks.

The evaluation attracted 30 registered teams from home and abroad, submitting a total of 155 evaluation systems. Participants increased compared with previous years in terms of both team and system numbers. The remainder of this paper introduces the evaluation plan, datasets, and results of all tasks in this campaign.

2   Evaluation Plan

2.1   Tasks in the Evaluation

The evaluation contains four tasks: bilingual translation, multilingual translation, speech translation and quality estimation. Each task is divided into different tracks according to language pairs and domains. The project settings are detailed in Table 1.

Table 1. CCMT 2019 tasks and tracks

Task	Track	Code	Direction
Bilingual translation task	Chinese-English news	CE	Chinese-English
	English-Chinese news	EC	English-Chinese
	Mongolian-Chinese daily language	MC	Mongolian-Chinese
	Tibetan-Chinese government documents	TC	Tibetan-Chinese
	Uyghur-Chinese news	UC	Uyghur-Chinese
Multilingual translation task	Japanese-Chinese-English Multilingual translation	JE	Japanese-English
Speech translation task	Chinese-English speech translation	SpeechCE	Chinese-English
Quality estimation	Word-level quality estimation	QE-Word	Chinese-English
	Sentence-level quality estimation	QE-S	English-Chinese

Among them, the translation tasks include Chinese-English news, English-Chinese news, Mongolian-Chinese daily language, Tibetan-Chinese government literature, and Uyghur-Chinese news. The multilingual translation task is a multilingual translation project in patent field between English, Japanese and Chinese. The speech translation task is a Chinese-English translation for reporting scenarios. The quality estimation task includes two tracks, word level and sentence level, covering quality estimation for Chinese-English and English-Chinese multi-domain translation.

Table 2. Statistics of the teams and corresponding tasks registered

Name	Task (Track)								
	CE	EC	MC	TC	UC	JE	Speech-CE	QE-Word	QE-S
NICT (National Institute of Information and Communications Technology)	✓	✓							
Peking University				✓					
Beihang University		✓	✓	✓	✓	O	O	✓	✓
Beijing Jiaotong University	✓	✓	✓	✓	✓	✓	O	✓	✓
Beijing Institute of Technology			✓	✓	✓				✓
Dalian University of Technology	✓	O				O			
Northeastern University								✓	✓
Heilongjiang University							✓		
Heilongjiang Institute of Technology	O	O						✓	✓
Hohhot University for Nationalities			✓						
Jiangxi Normal University	✓	✓							✓
Kunming University of Science and Technology	O	O	O	O	O		O		
Inner Mongolia University			✓						
Inner Mongolia Normal University			✓						
Shanghai Jiaotong University	✓	✓	✓	✓	✓	✓	✓	O	O
Soochow University					✓				
Xiamen University							✓	✓	✓
Xinjiang University	O	O					O	O	O
University of Science and Technology of China	✓	✓	✓	✓	✓	O	O		
Minzu University of China	✓	✓	✓	✓	✓	✓			
Nanjing Institute of Information Technology		✓			✓		O		
Institute of Computing Technology, Chinese Academy of Sciences				✓			✓		
Institute of Information Engineering, Chinese Academy of Sciences	O	O				✓			
Institute of Automation, Chinese Academy of Sciences			✓	✓	✓				
Institute of Intelligent Machinery, Chinese Academy of Sciences			✓						
Guangdong OPPO Mobile Telecommunications Corp., Ltd.	✓	✓	O	O	O	✓	O		
Huawei Technology Co., Ltd.	✓	✓							
Tencent Technology (Beijing) Co., Ltd.			✓	✓	✓				
Sinosoft Technology Co., Ltd.			✓	O	✓				
Global Tone Communication Technology Co., Ltd.	O	O	O	O	O	O	O		
Number of Registered Team	15	16	16	14	14	9	12	7	9
Number of System Submitted	18	20	26	21	27	13	7	5/4	7

* "√" means registered and submitted results successfully; "O" means registered without submission; "5/4" means that 5 submissions for Chinese-English and 4 submissions for English-Chinese in word-level quality estimation.

The evaluation campaign began on March 15th, 2019, and the deadline for the result submission is June 20, 2019. Participants in this evaluation are required to provide a system description[1] and a system technical report. The technical report will only be exchanged between the participants, and only several of them are accepted to be published in this volume of proceedings.

2.2   Participants

A total of 30 teams registered in the evaluation,[2] and a total of 155 system results were submitted, including 87 main system results and 71 comparison results. The so-called main system is assigned as the representative system by each team. The training data for the main system can only use those specified in Sect. 3. The comparison system can apply extra-training data not specified in the evaluation plan. Systems only using the training data specified are called restricted system, while those using extra-data are called unrestricted system.

Table 2 shows the details of each team with their registered tasks and total evaluation systems. In terms of team number, bilingual translation (i.e. CE, EC, MC, TC and UC) all received most attention. The new task of speech translation tasks also attracted a wide range of interests. As to the system submission, Mongolian-Chinese (MC), Uyghur-Chinese (UC) translations tasks received the most submissions. And the speech translation task received only 1/3 of the registered number.

3   Datasets

3.1   Bilingual Translation Task Datasets

The task includes five language pairs (CE, EC, MC, TC and UC) and three domains (news, daily language and government literature). All the files are UTF-8 encoded XML file. The development sets for each language pair consist of one reference answer. The test set for CE and EC consists of four references, and the test sets for MC, TC and UC consist of one reference. Reference are translated by professional translators independently.

The Chinese-English and English-Chinese tasks are jointly organized with WMT19, so the data provided by WMT19 can also be used in this task. To be specific, in addition to training set, development set and test set provided by CWMT 2018, WMT19 also allows the using of following data:

(1)   Chinese-English Parallel Corpus (News Commentary V13 and UN Parallel Corpus V1.0)

(2)   English and Chinese monolingual Corpus (Europarl v7/v8, News Commentary, Common Crawl, News Crawl, News Discussions, etc.); LDC for English and Gigaword for Chinese (LDC2011T07, LDC2009T13, LDC2007T07, LDC2009T27)

---

[1] https://ccmt2019.jxnu.edu.cn/page/main1923/CCMT2019_Evaluation_report.zip (in Chinese).

[2] One team can't be contacted after registration, which is not counted as in the 30 teams.

More details of the data sets can be found in Tables 3, 4 and 5.

Table 3. Details of CCMT 2019 bilingual translation task training set

Task	Scale (sentence bead)	Provider	Remarks
CE-EC translation task (news)	9,023,471	Datum Co., Ltd., NEU, ICT, CASIA	Parallel corpus
	5,281	ICT	Chinese sentence and four English reference translations
	8,665	ICT	English sentence and four Chinese reference translations
	4003	NJU	CWMT 2017 development set, test set
	11 M words	XMU	Chinese monolingual corpus
MC translation task (daily language)	262,644	IMU, IIM, ICT	Parallel corpus
TC translation task (government document)	157,959	QNU, XBMU, TU, XMU, ICT	Parallel corpus
UC translation task (news)	170,061	ICT, XTIPC of CAS	Parallel corpus

Table 4. Details of CCMT 2019 bilingual translation task development set

Task	Scale	Provider	Remarks
CE-EC translation task (news)	2481/1500	WMT 2018 test set	Single reference
MC translation task (daily language)	1000	IMU	Single reference
TC translation task (government document)	1000	QNU	Single reference
UC translation task (news)	1000	XTIPC of CAS	Single reference

Table 5. Details of CCMT 2019 bilingual translation task test set

Task	Scale	Provider	Remarks
CE translation task (news)	1011	NEU	Four references
EC translation task (news)	1000	NEU	Four references
MC translation task (daily language)	1001	IMU	Single reference
TC translation task (government document)	1000	QNU	Single reference
UC translation task (news)	1000	XTIPC.CAS	Single reference

3.2   Multilingual Translation Task Datasets

The training corpus for multilingual translation task includes two language pairs (Japanese-Chinese and Chinese-English) in the patent domain. All the files are UTF-8 encoded XML file. The development set and test set in this ask consist of one reference translation, which are translated by professional translators independently.

More details of the datasets can be found in Tables 6, 7 and 8.

Table 6. Details of CCMT 2019 multilingual translation task training set

Corpus	Scale	Provider
Japanese-Chinese (bilingual)	3,000,000	Lingosail Co., Ltd.
Chinese-English (bilingual)	3,000,000	
Chinese (monolingual)	7,114,700 (sentences)	

Table 7. Details of CCMT 2019 multilingual translation task development set

Corpus	Scale	Provider	Remarks
Japanese-Chinese	6,000	Lingosail Co., Ltd.	Single reference
Chinese-English	3,000		
Japanese-English	3,000		

Table 8. Details of CCMT 2019 multilingual translation task test set

Task	Scale	Provider	Remarks
Japnese-English	1217	Lingosail Co., Ltd.	Single reference

3.3   Speech Translation Task Datasets

The data of speech translation, namely Baidu Speech Translation Collection (BSTC), is provided by Baidu Company, which contains more than 50 h Mandarin acoustic speeches, and corresponding English translations. The speeches are collected from Chinese talk shows, such as Tndao, Zaojiu and technical reports from Baidu Company. One characteristic of this dataset is that it contains multiple domains, referring to Science, Economy, Startup, Education, etc.

The construction of this dataset is elaborated and labor-intensive:

(1) Each talk is carefully transcribed into Chinese by human translators. And the transcription contains accurate punctuations.
(2) The sentences in one talk are translated into English text rather than in a sentence-by-sentence manner.
(3) The utterance of source speech is segmented by the English translation and annotated with accurate timelines.

Table 9. The overall statistics of BSTC (CER means character error rate).

Dataset	Talks	Utterances	Transcription (Characters)	Translation (Words)	Duration (Hours)	CER	CER (5-best)
Train	174	26,533	796,679	2,292,025	50.57	17.32%	15.68%
Develop	16	956	26,059	75,074	1.58	15.21%	13.20%
Test	6	975	25,832	70,503	1.46	10.32%	8.57%

Moreover, the dataset also contains automatically transcribed Chinese text from a high-performance Automatic Speech Recognition (ASR) system. The overall statistics of this dataset is listed as follows (Table 9):

It is worth noting that the test data contains noisy ASR results and punctuations. The participants are freely to use the officially released data. But we encourage all participants to investigate novel methods to enhance the robustness of the translation model against noisy data.

Compared to conventional text-to-text translation task, the speech translation task is more difficult and challenging:

- The participants are required to handle the acoustic input rather than relatively simple text input if they propose to use an End-to-End model.
- The ASR results are error-prone, and the participants are required to develop novel methods to enhance the robustness of the translation model.
- The participants are also required to deal with the erroneously annotated punctuations.
- The participants are required to deal with the irregularities in each talk.
- The size of BSTC is relatively small, and the participants are required to use additional training corpus to improve the translation quality.

3.4 Quality Estimation Task Datasets

In CCMT 2019, this task is augmented with a new track: word-level translation quality estimation. Generally speaking, the datasets of this task contain two parts: one is the training set and development set with translation quality annotation provided by the organizer; the other is the Chinese-English and English-Chinese parallel data for auxiliary training the system.

The word-level quality estimation data is provided by Alibaba (China). Data (source sentence) comes from 6 scenarios: mostly from Alibaba's e-commerce and IT domains, partly from IT economy, politics, technology and daily conversation. The procedure of data generation is as follows:

- The translation of each original text is generated from 3 online translation engines (online translation service) and a neural network translation engine (provided by Alibaba). Duplicated translations are removed.
- All translations are edited by professional interpreters to get post-edit translations.

- Machine translated sentences are aligned with the post-editing version using TER toolkit,[3] with the following settings: tokenized, case insensitive, exactly matching only, disabling shifts by using the '-d 0' option. Accordingly, final OK/BAD labels for target words and gaps are determined.

Sentence-level track is again supported by Lingosail Co., Ltd. The dataset cover multi-fields, such as politics, finance, science and technology. The translation candidates comes from the learners using the Shiyibao (http://www.shiyibao.com/), as well as multiple online translation engines. Then the final translations are post-edited by professional translators, which enables the computation of HTER score. It should be noted that all the data released by CWMT 2018 (including the original development set and test set) has been further polished and updated in t2019. Therefore, the CWMT 2018 sentence-level quality estimation dataset will be officially discontinued.

More details of the datasets can be found in Tables 10 and 11.

Table 10. Details of CCMT 2019 word-level dataset

Task	Size	Provider
Training set (CE)	11039 (4606 source sentences)	Alibaba
Training set (EC)	10878 (4105 source sentences)	(China)
Development set (CE)	1050 (375 source sentences)	
Development set (EC)	1129 (375 source sentences)	
Test set (CE)	1093	
Test set (EC)	1122	

Table 11. Details of CCMT 2019 sentence-level dataset

Task	Size	Provider
Training set (CE)	10070 (2503 source sentences)	Lingosail Co., Ltd.
Training set (EC)	14789 (3043 source sentences)	
Development set (CE)	1143 (300 source sentences)	
Development set (EC)	1381 (300 source sentences)	
Test set (CE)	1385	
Test set (EC)	1445	

4   Results

CCMT 2019 continues to emphasize its research nature, and all evaluation results are for research purpose only. No participant is authorized to cite the following results or disclose the identity of any participant in commercial activities. For this purpose, this report replace the name of the participant by an anonymous ID. In this section, we present the results of the top 10 system performances for each task, as well as the

---

[3] http://www.cs.umd.edu/~ snover/tercom/.

significance test results. For the description of each submitted system, please refer to the appendix of this report[4].

4.1   Bilingual Translation Task: Between Chinese and English

In the English-Chinese and Chinese-English news translation task, a total of 11 teams submitted their system results, as shown in Tables 12, 13, 14 and 15.

Table 12. CCMT 2019 Chinese-English translation results of main systems

	BLEU4-SBP	BLEU4	NIST5	GTM	mWER	mPER	ICT	METEOR	TER
ce-S16-primary	0.5554	0.5636	11.7661	0.8619	0.4370	0.3111	0.5035	0.3450	0.4135
ce-S4-primary	0.4778	0.5015	10.8763	0.8164	0.5015	0.3602	0.4825	0.3135	0.4571
ce-S17-primary	0.4768	0.4785	10.4683	0.8454	0.4766	0.3517	0.4014	0.2605	0.5897
*ce-S10-primary	0.4730	0.4859	10.8290	0.8208	0.5099	0.3595	0.4550	0.2444	0.5672
ce-S6-primary	0.4367	0.4394	10.0143	0.8230	0.5160	0.3715	0.3775	0.2424	0.6098
ce-S2-primary	0.4286	0.4388	10.1852	0.7980	0.5379	0.3860	0.4103	0.3030	0.4963
ce-S14-primary	0.4145	0.4404	10.0250	0.7828	0.5601	0.4073	0.4217	0.2913	0.5049
ce-S19-primary	0.3559	0.3760	9.0710	0.7326	0.5948	0.4436	0.3704	0.2606	0.5412
ce-S8-primary	0.3239	0.3515	8.1149	0.6665	0.6389	0.5011	0.3554	0.2407	0.5773
ce-S18-primary	0.2975	0.3149	8.0927	0.6936	0.6466	0.4844	0.3201	0.2363	0.5803

* indicating a delayed submission.

Table 13. Significance test for main systems in CCMT 2019 Chinese-English track (● significant, ○ not significant, with $p < 0.05$)

	ce2019-S16-primary	ce-S4-primary	ce-S17-primary	ce-S10-primary	ce-S6-primary	ce-S2-primary	ce-S14-primary	ce-S19-primary	ce-S8-primary	ce-S18-primary
ce-S16-primary	–	●	●	●	●	●	●	●	●	●
ce-S4-primary	●	–	○	○	●	●	●	●	●	●
ce-S17-primary	●	○	–	○	●	●	●	●	●	●
ce-S10-primary	●	○	○	–	●	●	●	●	●	●
ce-S6-primary	●	●	●	●	–	○	○	●	●	●
ce-S2-primary	●	●	●	●	○	–	○	●	●	●
ce-S14-primary	●	●	●	●	●	○	–	●	●	●
ce-S19-primary	●	●	●	●	●	●	●	–	●	●
ce-S8-primary	●	●	●	●	●	●	●	●	–	●
ce-S18-primary	●	●	●	●	●	●	●	●	●	–

---

[4] Available only in Chinese via https://ccmt2019.jxnu.edu.cn/page/main1923/CCMT2019_Evaluation_report.zip.

Table 14. CCMT 2019 English-Chinese results of main systems

	BLEU5-SBP	BLEU5	BLEU6	NIST6	NIST7	GTM	mWER	mPER	ICT	METEOR	TER
ec-S16-primary	0.6727	0.6910	0.6445	13.5650	13.6160	0.8932	0.3256	0.2179	0.6019	0.5672	0.2698
ec-S6-primary	0.6324	0.6457	0.5976	13.1110	13.1560	0.8844	0.3635	0.2378	0.5480	0.5502	0.3062
*ec-S10-primary	0.6198	0.6345	0.5851	13.0330	13.0760	0.8834	0.3743	0.2438	0.5393	0.5435	0.3114
ec-S17-primary	0.5625	0.5714	0.5201	12.2340	12.2700	0.8620	0.4102	0.2740	0.4737	0.5281	0.3475
ec-S8-primary	0.5537	0.5881	0.5360	11.9330	11.9680	0.8387	0.4187	0.2888	0.5253	0.5145	0.3509
ec-S19-primary	0.5423	0.5652	0.5112	12.0810	12.1150	0.8459	0.4273	0.2829	0.4842	0.5133	0.3539
*ec-S31-primary	0.5222	0.5529	0.4974	11.7770	11.8090	0.8360	0.4389	0.2935	0.4811	0.5059	0.3627
ec-S2-primary	0.4666	0.4858	0.4295	11.1510	11.1750	0.8125	0.5006	0.3294	0.4133	0.4722	0.4158
ec-S18-primary	0.4469	0.4753	0.4208	10.4960	10.5200	0.7828	0.5021	0.3552	0.4080	0.4489	0.4252
ec-S14-primary	0.4332	0.4521	0.3985	10.0560	10.0780	0.7836	0.5179	0.3585	0.4461	0.4600	0.4272

* indicating a delayed submission.

Table 15. Significance test for main systems in CCMT 2019 English- Chinese track (● significant, ○ not significant, with $p < 0.05$)

	ec-S16-primary	ec-S6-primary	ec-S10-primary	ec-S17-primary	ec-S8-primary	ec-S19-primary	ec-S31-primary	ec-S2-primary	ec-S18-primary	ec-S14-primary
ec-S16-primary	–	●	●	●	●	●	●	●	●	●
ec-S6-primary	●	–	○	●	●	●	●	●	●	●
ec-S10-primary	●	○	–	●	●	●	●	●	●	●
ec-S17-primary	●	●	●	–	○	●	●	●	●	●
ec-S8-primary	●	●	●	○	–	●	●	●	●	●
ec-S19-primary	●	●	●	●	●	–	●	●	●	●
ec-S31-primary	●	●	●	●	●	●	–	●	●	●
ec-S2-primary	●	●	●	●	●	●	●	–	●	●
ec-S18-primary	●	●	●	●	●	●	●	●	–	○
ec-S14-primary	●	●	●	●	●	●	●	●	○	–

(1) Translation Model and System Implementation

All systems in these two tracks were based on transformer. S16 used relative attention to model the position information, and its experiment indicates that this method can achieve 1.64 BLEU improvement on Chinese-English task and 0.79 BLEU improvement on English-Chinese task.

In addition, S10 investigated the different initialization of the parameters of the Transformer model. The BERT embedding and the word embedding were both applied with the following findings:

- BERT embedding is not suitable for the initialization of the Encoder layer of the Transformer model
- Pre-trained embedding does not significantly improve the performance of the Transformer model

As for the implementation of translation system, S19 chose the MXNET, S6 and S17 the Marianm, and S8, S4 and S14 the THUMT (the open source neural machine translation toolkit by Tsinghua University). The rest of the submissions is powered by Tensor2Tensor (Google) or FairSeq (Facebook).

As mentioned above, all teams chose the Transformer architecture, while in last CWMT 2018, 10 participants used Transformer-based NMT system, and one of them used the SMT system based on the hierarchical phrase model in system integration.

(2) Data Cleaning and Pre-processing

For the selection of training data, 8 participants only used CCMT 2019 data, the remaining participants also used WMT18 (S16), WMT19 (S17) and non-publicly available bilingual data (S31 unrestricted system). Data preprocessing usually involves the following steps: Chinese word segmentation, full-width/half-width Chinese character conversion, tokenization, abnormal word filtering, sentences filtering by length and alignment ratio. It is claimed that the data cleaning and preprocessing are positive to translation quality of the submitted systems.

When processing Chinese, S16 carried out a more detailed filtering processing based on the alignment model, the translation model and the language model. In addition, S10 simply split Chinese into characters, for which they reported a comparable results with that of Chinese word segmentation.

(3) Out-of-Vocabulary Words and Named Entity

In these shared tasks, all participants adopted BPE to alleviate OOV issue. In addition, S4 and S31 further adopted label-post-processing technique for named entities and such special words as date, time, URL, etc. In their systems, the OOV words and named entities in training corpus are first identified by an independent named entity recognition model or rule-based method. Then the entities are replaced with predefined tags in an entities-tag dictionary. In addition, the method also constructed a translation dictionary based on the alignment information. In the decoding phase, the target tag is detected for its corresponding source tag by the alignment information, and then replaced with the corresponding translation. It is claimed that this method could improve the readability of the translation, while the BLEU score increase is trivial.

(4) Model Training

The optimizer for Transformer model is Adam. All systems use the parameter settings of Transformer-base or Transformer-big mentioned in (Vaswani et al. 2017). S10 also explored the number of network layers, and their results showed that increasing the depth of the network can bring an improvement in model performance.

In addition, when training the model, six teams used back translation to form a pseudo-parallel corpus. For example, S16 iteratively used back translation in Chinese-English and English-Chinese translation tasks, which further improves the model performance. At the same time, their report also pointed out that although this method can improve the performance by about 3 BLEU, the effective iteration in this method is limited to the first two rounds. After three rounds, the iterative back translation method can hardly bring about any improvement.

(5) Re-ranking

During beam search, different features can be used to score and re-rank candidate translations. In Chinese-English and English-Chinese translation task, re-ranking is usually based on the following features:

- Translation probabilities from Decoder
- Translation probabilities from Right-left Decoder
- Pre-trained language model score
- Translation coverage score
- Translation quality estimation score

The re-ranking model can be further trained on the development set using MIRA. S6 used S4 both reported 1.1 BLEU increase resulted from 4 features based re-ranking within a beam size of 10.

(6) System Ensemble

There are 7 teams in Chinese-English translation, and 6 in English-Chinese translation adopted the model fusion technique. All candidate systems for fusion are NMT systems. It is reported that the greater the difference between candidate models, the more improvement could be brought by this method.

(7) Other Techniques Observed

S10 used multi-task training. They jointly trained machine translation and corpus classification and reported 1.36 BLEU increase. They argued that this method could achieve better results owing to the fact that there are large differences in the quality, field, and style of different training corpora: directly merging different corpora may bring improper data distribution.

4.2 Bilingual Translation Task: From Mongolian, Tibetan and Uyghur into Chinese

The CCMT 2019 evaluation results for Mongolian-Chinese, Tibetan-Chinese, and Uyghur-Chinese are detailed from Table 16, 17, 18, 19, 20 and 21.

Table 16. CCMT 2019 Mongolian-Chines results of main systems (top 10 only)

	BLEU5-SBP	BLEU5	BLEU6	NIST6	NIST7	GTM	mWER	mPER	ICT	METEOR	TER
mc-S32-primary	0.6206	0.6356	0.6151	10.8730	10.881	0.8108	0.2846	0.2271	0.6059	0.7518	0.2627
mc-S24-primary	0.5882	0.6179	0.5967	10.3980	10.405	0.7902	0.3224	0.2588	0.5657	0.7345	0.2968
mc-S33-primary	0.4891	0.5083	0.4754	9.7963	9.8042	0.7624	0.3674	0.2861	0.5389	0.6759	0.3374
mc-S29-primary	0.4698	0.4961	0.4692	9.1621	9.1678	0.7150	0.4237	0.3432	0.4697	0.6368	0.3910
#mc-S13-primary	0.4631	0.4825	0.4545	9.1907	9.1985	0.7181	0.4198	0.3341	0.4593	0.6304	0.3871
mc-S8-primary	0.4456	0.4620	0.4308	9.1537	9.1612	0.7198	0.4186	0.3317	0.4508	0.6236	0.3843
##mc-S3-primary	0.4203	0.4422	0.4112	8.6380	8.6451	0.6916	0.4500	0.3615	0.4159	0.5999	0.4180
mc-S16-primary	0.4176	0.4435	0.4113	8.7181	8.7245	0.6987	0.4536	0.3609	0.4161	0.6062	0.4188
mc-S22-primary	0.3610	0.3813	0.3501	7.9715	7.9772	0.6489	0.5171	0.4140	0.3742	0.5453	0.4764
mc-S9-primary	0.3584	0.3797	0.3533	7.7629	7.7690	0.6324	0.5310	0.4344	0.3624	0.5307	0.4952

unrestricted system, # system condition unclear

Table 17. Significance test for main systems in CCMT 2019 Mongolian-Chinese track (● significant, ○ not significant, with $p < 0.05$)

	mc-S32-primary	mc-S24-primary	mc-S33-primary	mc-S29-primary	mc-S13-primary	mc-S8-primary	mc-S3-primary_a	mc-S16-primary	mc-S22-primary	mc-S9-primary
mc-S32-primary	–	●	●	●	●	●	●	●	●	●
mc-S24-primary	●	–	○	●	●	●	●	●	●	●
mc-S33-primary	●	○	–	●	●	●	●	●	●	●
mc-S29-primary	●	●	●	–	○	●	○	●	●	●
mc-S13-primary	●	●	●	○	–	○	●	○	●	●
mc-S8-primary	●	●	●	●	○	–	●	●	●	●
mc_2019_S3_primary_a	●	●	●	○	●	●	–	○	●	●
mc-S16-primary	●	●	●	●	○	●	○	–	●	●
mc-S22-primary	●	●	●	●	●	●	●	●	–	●
mc-S9-primary	●	●	●	●	●	●	●	●	●	–

Table 18. CCMT 2019 Tibetan-Chinese results of main systems

	BLEU5-SBP	BLEU5	BLEU6	NIST6	NIST7	GTM	mWER	mPER	ICT	METEOR	TER
tc-S26-primary	0.6221	0.6441	0.6153	10.8120	10.8450	0.8310	0.2735	0.2064	0.6045	0.7815	0.2441
tc-S24-primary	0.6038	0.6221	0.5943	10.6070	10.6390	0.8146	0.2940	0.2245	0.5996	0.7608	0.2645
tc-S16-primary	0.5831	0.6075	0.5745	10.3940	10.4240	0.8138	0.3079	0.2278	0.5656	0.7609	0.2712
tc-S8-primary	0.5796	0.5930	0.5649	10.4150	10.4460	0.8016	0.3128	0.2420	0.5871	0.7381	0.2828
tc-S32-primary	0.5562	0.5826	0.5488	10.1680	10.1990	0.7980	0.3331	0.2491	0.5359	0.7361	0.2965
tc-S9-primary	0.5266	0.5529	0.5232	9.6544	9.6849	0.7621	0.3771	0.2868	0.5075	0.7002	0.3390
tc-S18-primary	0.4945	0.5067	0.4790	9.3536	9.3810	0.7462	0.3989	0.3079	0.5223	0.6675	0.3601
tc-S14-primary	0.4471	0.4655	0.4278	9.1599	9.1851	0.7401	0.4191	0.3139	0.4610	0.6528	0.3754
tc-S12-primary	0.4442	0.4494	0.4094	9.1318	9.1584	0.7590	0.3857	0.2963	0.5210	0.6552	0.3467
tc-S19-primary	0.4205	0.4489	0.4095	8.6853	8.7095	0.7183	0.4575	0.3448	0.4310	0.6352	0.4093

Table 19. Significance test for main systems in CCMT 2019 Tibetan-Chinese track (● significant, ○ not significant, with $p < 0.05$)

	tc-S26-primary	tc-S24-primary	tc-S16-primary	tc-S8-primary	tc-S32-primary	tc-S9-primary	tc-S18-primary	tc-S14-primary	tc-S12-primary	tc-S19-primary
tc-S26-primary	–	●	●	●	●	●	●	●	●	●
tc-S24-primary	●	–	○	●	●	●	●	●	●	●
tc-S16-primary	●	○	–	○	●	●	●	●	●	●
tc-S8-primary	●	●	○	–	●	●	●	●	●	●
tc-S32-primary	●	●	●	●	–	●	●	●	●	●
tc-S9-primary	●	●	●	●	●	–	●	●	●	●
tc-S18-primary	●	●	●	●	●	●	–	○	○	○
tc-S14-primary	●	●	●	●	●	●	○	–	●	○
tc-S12-primary	●	●	●	●	●	●	○	●	–	●
tc-S19-primary	●	●	●	●	●	●	○	○	●	–

(1) Translation Model

The systems submitted by all teams are dominated by transformer. The top-ranked S26 in Tibetan-Chinese track is a classical Transformer framework. In contrast, S32 which top-ranked in the both Mongolian-Chinese track and Uyghur-Chinese track, proposed a new variant of Transformer: a data weighting mechanism was added to the model in addition to some modifications of model parameters and activation functions.

Table 20. CCMT 2019 Uyghur-Chinese results of main systems (top 10 only)

	BLEU5-SBP	BLEU5	BLEU6	NIST6	NIST7	GTM	mWER	mPER	ICT	METEOR	TER
uc-S32-primary	0.4808	0.5015	0.4579	10.4550	10.468	0.7847	0.3622	0.2621	0.4406	0.6994	0.3221
uc-S24-primary	0.4694	0.4850	0.4413	10.3930	10.406	0.7798	0.3664	0.2653	0.4412	0.6878	0.3263
uc-S11-primary	0.4567	0.4713	0.4269	10.2660	10.278	0.7727	0.3742	0.2724	0.4313	0.6773	0.3341
uc-S16-primary	0.4349	0.4511	0.4064	10.0040	10.016	0.7583	0.3985	0.2895	0.4095	0.6607	0.3561
uc-S9-primary	0.4305	0.4417	0.3990	9.9484	9.9605	0.7541	0.4034	0.2959	0.4247	0.6490	0.3610
uc-S8-primary	0.4067	0.4194	0.3756	9.6760	9.6882	0.7418	0.4179	0.3077	0.3961	0.6319	0.3760
##uc-S3-primary	0.3955	0.4154	0.3708	9.3559	9.3670	0.7281	0.4498	0.3232	0.3616	0.6272	0.4002
uc-S14-primary	0.3817	0.3991	0.3567	9.2953	9.3066	0.7182	0.4691	0.3407	0.3754	0.6103	0.4169
uc-S19-primary	0.3336	0.3520	0.3073	8.6522	8.6604	0.6876	0.5059	0.3696	0.3143	0.5726	0.4548
uc-S31-primary	0.3049	0.3175	0.2773	8.1391	8.1477	0.6501	0.5478	0.4089	0.3036	0.5273	0.4966

unrestricted system

Table 21. Significance test for main systems in CCMT 2019 Uyghur-Chinese track (● significant, ○ not significant, with $p < 0.05$)

	uc-S32-primary	uc-S24-primary	uc-S11-primary	uc-S16-primary	uc-S9-primary	uc-S8-primary	uc-S3-primary	uc-S14-primary	uc-S19-primary	uc-S31-primary
uc-S32-primary	–	●	●	●	●	●	●	●	●	●
uc-S24-primary	●	–	●	●	●	●	●	●	●	●
uc-S11-primary	●	●	–	●	●	●	●	●	●	●
uc-S16-primary	●	●	●	–	○	●	●	●	●	●
uc-S9-primary	●	●	●	○	–	●	●	●	●	●
uc-S8-primary	●	●	●	●	●	–	●	●	●	●
uc-S3-primary	●	●	●	●	●	●	–	●	●	●
uc-S14-primary	●	●	●	●	●	●	●	–	●	●
uc-S19-primary	●	●	●	●	●	●	●	●	–	●
uc-S31-primary*	●	●	●	●	●	●	●	●	●	–

* indicating a delayed submission.

In the Mongolian-Chinese track, S33 also adopted a Transformer variant (CNN + GLU) which introduced CNN and gating units into the input layer and encoder of Transformer. S22 jointly trained the Transformer encoder and decoder for both machine translation and language modeling. S16 reported that the relative attention brought about 1 BLEU improvement. S3 revealed that the Marian were better than OpenNMT and Fairseq on the given task.

In the Uyghur-Chinese track, S11 applied convolutional neural networks Light-Conv and DynamicConv, and claimed a better performance than transformer in the experiments. RNN search model can only be observed as a candidate for system ensemble.

(2) Corpus Processing and Back Translation

A common practice for the above 3 tracks is corpus processing, including tokenization and normalization, sentence filtering and deduplication. Almost all teams applied the BPE algorithm to reduce the impact of OOV on model performance. Since all the three track are severely challenged by the low-resource issue: much less training corpus are provided compared with that between Chinese and English. Another common practice for the above teams are back translation.

Substantial efforts were made on how to find the most favorable pseudo-data for the model training. S32, top-ranked in Mongolian-Chinese and Uighur-Chinese track, regarded this issue as a text classification problem: applying N-gram language model and BERT pre-training model to score the generated sentence pairs. Similarly, S26 that ranks top in the Tibetan-Chinese track, uses a decreasing strategy: back translation was reduced gradually until only the real bilingual corpus is applied. Results show that these strategies have a positive impact on translation quality.

In addition to back translation, some participants have tried other data augmentation methods. For example, S24 used knowledge distillation to construct pseudo data: combining translation and decoding direction, four teacher models were constructed to decode a batch of pseudo data. The experiment showed that this method was not always successful: achieving significant improvements in Mongolian-Chinese and Uighur-Chinese while no gains in Tibetan-Chinese.

(3) System Ensemble

The technique of system ensemble were adopted by most teams except S14. Most of the teams reported only the technique they chose, but some teams (such as S19, S26, etc.) presented a further comparison of the available methods. Generally speaking, they claimed that the parameter average technique was less recommended, and the differences between candidate models was a key issue to performance improvement.

4.3   Multilingual Translation Task

Despite the pivot translation nature of this task, all submission systems used transformer again and results are shown in Tables 22 and 23.

Table 22. CCMT 2019 multilingual translation task (Japanese-English) results of main systems

	BLEU5-SBP	BLEU5	BLEU6	NIST6	NIST7	GTM	mWER	mPER	ICT	METEOR	TER
je-S6-primary	0.4575	0.4737	0.4249	9.6072	9.6425	0.7823	0.427	0.2591	0.4026	0.6402	0.3954
##je-S18-primary	0.4317	0.4509	0.3999	9.4626	9.4931	0.7715	0.4517	0.2707	0.4032	0.5711	0.5055
je-S15-primary	0.3453	0.3692	0.3177	8.3575	8.3760	0.7108	0.5158	0.3538	0.3303	0.5101	0.5851
je-S19-primary	0.3359	0.3480	0.2987	7.8589	7.8752	0.6999	0.5255	0.3585	0.3063	0.5135	0.5945
*je-S14-primary	0.3007	0.3293	0.2810	7.5679	7.5833	0.6618	0.5811	0.4233	0.3164	0.4542	0.6739
je-S8-primary	0.1436	0.1566	0.1255	4.2457	4.2507	0.4735	0.7570	0.6342	0.1791	0.2996	1.0397

* indicates that it was not submitted in time, ## indicates that it is an unrestricted system

Table 23. Significance test for main systems in CCMT 2019 multilingual translation task (● significant, ○ not significant, with $p < 0.05$)

	je-S6-primary	je-S18-primary	je-S15-primary	je-S19-primary	je-S14-primary	je-S8-primary
je-S6-primary	–	●	●	●	●	●
je-S18-primary	●	–	●	●	●	●
je-S15-primary	●	●	–	●	●	●
je-S19-primary	●	●	●	–	●	●
je-S14-primary	●	●	●	●	–	●
je-S8-primary	●	●	●	●	●	–

In this task, the top-ranked S6 reported that the transformer-big brought 1.19 BLEU improvement than the transformer-base model, and the 8 layers self-attention performed better than 16 layers by 0.48 BLEU score. Other techniques including corpus processing, re-ranking and system ensemble were again observed, which will not be discussed in detail here.

4.4　Speech Translation Evaluation

In CCMT 2019 evaluation campaign, we proposed a new task to boost the research on speech translation. The participants are encouraged to investigate novel methods to improve translation quality (e.g., End-to-End model and robust translation model). Finally, we received seven submissions from four participants before the deadline. Nevertheless, there are eight participants without any submissions in this year's campaign.

We also train two baseline systems for comparison:

- We use an open source toolkit[5] to segment Chinese text, and use Moses toolkit[6] to tokenize English text.
- We run the open source toolkit[7] to perform the BPE, and set the vocabulary size to 20,000 and 18,000 for Chinese and English, respectively.
- We pre-train a model using bilingual corpus from Chinese-English News translation task, namely baseline1. To train the model we use the open source toolkit, PaddlePaddle NMT[8].
- We finetune the pre-trained model on the BSTC corpus, namely baseline2.

We run the official evaluation scripts, and obtain the final results (Table 24):

Table 24. Evaluation results of speech translation task.

Submissions	BLEU4-SBP	BLEU4	NIST5	GTM	mWER	mPER	ICT	METEOR
S23.contrast.b.result	0.2035	0.2077	6.9964	0.699	0.7755	0.3216	0.0508	0.2286
S23.primary.a.result	0.2008	0.204	6.8736	0.6942	0.7813	0.3262	0.0482	0.2281
S23.contrast.c.result	0.1731	0.1731	6.6457	0.6607	0.7995	0.3652	0.0457	0.212
S26.primary.result	0.1713	0.1725	6.4415	0.6618	0.7935	0.3656	0.0327	0.2308
baseline2.result	0.1299	0.1299	6.0234	0.6229	0.8203	0.3994	0.0353	0.2646
S1.primary.result	0.1259	0.1292	5.9213	0.6195	0.846	0.4132	0.0277	0.2074
baseline1.result	0.1129	0.1129	5.3463	0.5882	0.8345	0.4361	0.0198	0.2682
S18.primary.result	0.1044	0.1044	5.1465	0.5746	0.8545	0.4506	0.0192	0.2577
S23.contrast.d.result	0.0134	0.0143	1.4384	0.2349	0.9688	0.827	0.0035	0.0608

As the above table shows, one contrastive submission from S23 achieves the best result measured by BLEU score. However, the ASR results in this submission is not from the officially released dataset. Instead they use a non-steaming ASR model to recognize the acoustic speech, and obtain a better ASR result. However, their primary submission still obtains the best result among all submissions.

In addition, both S23 and S26 significantly beat the baseline system, which indicates that the methods utilized in their models are effective and practical. However, we don't evaluate the latency for each submission due to the relatively small size of submissions, as well as the fact that all participants don't develop the simultaneous translation method.

There is no surprise that all participants used the cascaded method to finish the task due to the difficulty of using small size of training corpus to obtain a promising result for an End-to-End speech translation model. In details, the comparison of each submission can be summarized in Table 25.

---

[5] https://github.com/fxsjy/jieba.

[6] https://github.com/moses-smt/mosesdecoder/blob/master/scripts/tokenizer/tokenizer.perl.

[7] https://github.com/tensorflow/tensor2tensor/blob/master/tensor2tensor/data_generators/text_encoder_build_subword.py.

[8] https://github.com/paddlepaddle/paddle.

Table 25. Description of methods for each submissions

Submissions	Pre-processing	Data augmentation	Domain adaptation	Robust technologies	Ensemble
S23	✓	✓	✓	✓	✓
S26	✓	✓	✓	✓	✓
Baseline	✓	✗	✓	✗	✗
S18	○	○	○	○	○
S1	○	○	○	○	○

○ indicates that the methods for this submission is unknown

Pre-processing: Both S23 and XMU pre-processed the training and test data to improve the translation quality, such as normalizing the special characters, filtering the repeated sentences and low-quality sentence pairs, etc. For Chinese segmentation, S26 used the open source toolkit developed by Tsinghua University,[9] and S23 used the toolkit developed by Stanford University.[10] Both of them adopted the byte pair encoding (BPE) to encode the bilingual sentences.

Data Augmentation: Both S23 and S26 utilized the back-translation method to improve the performance and explore the monolingual data in Chinese-English News translation task.

Domain Adaptation: To finetune the model, S26 proposed to augment the training corpus in BSTC. They collect five results (5-best) from the ASR model for each utterance, and then generate additional bilingual sentences using identical English translation. While the S23 firstly finetune the model on the training data in BSTC, and then augment the finetuning corpus. Specifically, they collect the English sentences in the training corpus, and back translates them to obtain bilingual pairs. According to the final results, the method used by XMU is more effective.

Robust Technologies: The ICT propose a method to enhance the robustness of their model by augmenting the training corpus. In details, they propose multiple operations to add noise in the Chinese text:

- Randomly insert modal particle.
- Randomly repeat word.
- Randomly remove word.
- Randomly replace punctuation.
- Randomly replace word by its homophone.

Ensemble: Both ICT and XMU run six individual systems, and ensemble them to obtain further improvement. According to their descriptions, this technology significantly improves the translation quality.

---

[9] http://thulac.thunlp.org/.

[10] https://nlp.stanford.edu/software/segmenter.shtml.

4.5   Quality Estimation: Word Level Track

A total of 7 teams submitted the system for the word level track of translation quality estimation task, as shown in Tables 26 and 27. Table 28 further compares the methods of each system.

Table 26. CCMT 2019 word level translation quality estimation results: word choice

		F1_MULT	F1_OK	F1_BAD
Chinese-English	QE-Word-CE-S28	0.5257	0.8743	0.6012
	QE-Word-CE-S21	0.4688	0.8689	0.5395
	QE-Word-CE-S8	0.4156	0.8314	0.4999
	QE-Word-CE-S27	0.4050	0.8501	0.4765
	QE-Word-CE-S19	0.3970	0.7730	0.5137
English-Chinese	QE-Word-EC-S28	0.4236	0.8990	0.4712
	QE-Word-EC-S21	0.3380	0.8763	0.3857
	QE-Word-EC-S19	0.3336	0.8735	0.3819
	QE-Word-EC-S27	0.2867	0.9023	0.3177

Table 27. CCMT 2019 word level translation quality estimation results: translation gap

		F1_MULT	F1_OK	F1_BAD
Chinese-English	QE-Word-CE-S28	0.2579	0.9615	0.2683
	QE-Word-CE-S21	0.1713	0.9435	0.1816
	QE-Word-CE-S27	0.1173	0.9759	0.1202
	QE-Word-CE-S8	0.1015	0.9753	0.1041
	QE-Word-CE-S19	0.0565	0.9790	0.0577
English-Chinese	QE-Word-EC-S28	0.2003	0.9728	0.2060
	QE-Word-EC-S21	0.0960	0.9690	0.0991
	QE-Word-EC-S27	0.0350	0.9864	0.0355
	QE-Word-EC-S19	0	0.9871	0

From the evaluation results, it can be illustrated that translation gap prediction of quality estimation is more difficult than translation word prediction quality estimation, and the quality estimation of English-Chinese translation is more difficult than that of Chinese-English translation. The S28 submitted system outperform other teams. Compared with other systems, S28 was featured by the following techniques: Byte pair encoding (BPE) method was applied; the transformer model with two different directions (left to right & right to left) is used for feature extraction; and the ensemble of multiple model results leads to further improvement of the model performance.

Table 28. Techniques in QE-Word systems

Model architecture	S28	S21	S8	S27	S19
	Extractor-Estimator	Tansformer + LSTM	Extractor-Estimator	Extractor-Estimator	Extractor-Estimator
Byligual pre-training	✓	–	✓	✓	✓
Monoligual pre-training	✗	–	✗	✗	✗
Data expansion	✓	✓	✓	✓	✓
Word granularity	Sub-word	Word	Word	Word	Word
Ensemble	✓	–	–	–	–
Multi-task learning	✗	✗	✗	✗	✗

– unclear according to the system report submitted.

According the system descriptions, most of the teams employed the framework of Extractor-Estimator. The top-ranked S28 adopted the Transformer-DLCL as the Extractor, combining l2r and r2l translation models as the feature extractor. Its estimator was based on the bidirectional GRU model structure to carry out label prediction. The exception is S21, who performed quality estimation based on two-layer block Transformer and bidirectional LSTM.

Almost all teams used extra bilingual data to pre-train the model. S28 used 11M parallel sentence pairs provided by WMT 2019 and 5.5M pseudo data for pre-training. Its joint QE training uses 10K real data provided by CCMT 2019 and pseudo data obtained by TERCOM using 50K bilingual data. S21 additionally used the machine translation training data in the news field offered by CCMT 2019. S8 used UN English and Chinese corpus and CCMT 2019 English and Chinese machine translation corpus in the pre-training stage, totaling about 18 million. S27 filtered the translated news corpus provided by CCMT and related Chinese-English parallel corpus, and then mixed them with 10 times of CCMT QE corpus to obtain 10,498 million parallel sentence pairs to pre-trains the model. S19 uses an additional 3 million Chinese and English parallel sentence pairs to build a lexical dictionary.

Compared with WMT 2019, in which the word level quality estimation tasks include English-Russian and English-German, the number of participating teams is close. But, in terms of model structure, most of WMT19's participating teams used Bert Language Model (Masked LM) for pre-training, achieving relatively excellent QE performance. While in CCMT, all the contestants still use the structure of RNN or Transformer of previous years.

4.6 Quality Estimation: Sentence Level Track

In this track, CCMT 2019 received 7 submissions and the final results are listed in Table 29.

Table 29. CCMT 2019 sentence level translation quality estimation results

		Pearson r	RMSE	MAE	Spearman
Chinese-English	QE-Sent-CE-S28	0.6132	0.1159	0.0801	0.4730
	QE-Sent-CE-S2	0.5111	0.1296	0.0951	0.4230
	QE-Sent-CE-S21	0.4889	0.1292	0.0947	0.4075
	QE-Sent-CE-S27	0.4616	0.1745	0.1257	0.4153
	QE-Sent-CE-S8	0.4215	0.1423	0.0881	0.4090
	*QE-Sent-CE-S25	0.2566	0.1641	0.1155	0.1861
	QE-Sent-CE-S19	0.2048	0.1856	0.1492	0.2212
English-Chinese	QE-Sent-EC-S28	0.4288	0.1259	0.0914	0.2994
	QE-Sent-EC-S2	0.3573	0.1579	0.1324	0.3141
	QE-Sent-EC-S21	0.3541	0.1472	0.1114	0.2656
	QE-Sent-EC-S8	0.2601	0.1424	0.0923	0.1943
	QE-Sent-EC-S27	0.2356	0.1644	0.1151	0.2113
	*QE-Sent-EC-S25	0.1901	0.1442	0.1099	0.1107
	QE-Sent-EC-S19	−0.0070	0.1996	0.1607	0.0383

* a delayed submission

Compared with two submissions for this track last year, the top performance of the 7 teams (0.613) is nearly double the best result (0.31) of last year. Compared with the SVM based approach of last year, the submitted systems of this year all adopted deep neural models. The Extractor-Estimator framework has already become the state-of-the-art solutions to this track. A summary of the system features are presented in Table 30.

Table 30. Techniques adopted by sentence-level QE system

Model architecture	S28	S2	S21	S27	S8	S25	S19
	Extractor-Estimator	RNN + RNN RNN + CNN	Extractor-Estimator	Extractor-Estimator	BERT + LSTM	Extractor-Estimator	Predictor-Estimator
Bilingual pre-training	✓	✗	✓	✓	✗	✓	✓
Monolingual pre-training	✗	✓	✓	✗	✓	✗	✗
Data augmentation	✓	✓	✗	✓	✗	✗	✗
Word granularity	Sub-word	Sub-word	Word	Word	Word	Word	–
Ensemble	✓	✓	✓	–	–	–	–
Multi-task learning	✗	✗	✓	✗	✗	✗	✗

– unclear according to the system reports submitted.

The top-rank S28 applied the same techniques as in word level QE track: Transformer-DLCL as the Extractor, a combination of translation model of l2r with that of r2l to extract features, and the Bi-GRU as Estimator. The system submitted by S2 consisted of RNN-based feature extractor and RNN or CNN-based quality estimator. This team didn't use large-scale parallel corpus for pre-training, but use QE training data directly. BERT can also be observed in the submissions. S2 and S21 took the outputs of BERT as features into the model, while S8 used BERT as the main part of the model, on which they fine-turned by QE data. As for the data augmentation, S28 used back-translation to construct a large number of bilingual parallel corpora, and constructs a batch of translation quality estimation pseudo data through the translation system with real bilingual parallel corpus. S27 converted word-level data into sentence-level data to improve model training. Other techniques such as BPE and model ensemble were also reported with positive results according to submissions of the teams.

In general, the sentence level track of quality estimation of CCMT 2019 is somewhat in parallel to that of WMT 2019: with similar number of participants, similar Estimator-Extractor framework, and similar techniques like pre-training, BPE and so on. There are no prominent new attempts to this task in terms of model architecture or training techniques.

5 Conclusion

CCMT machine translation evaluation series have attracted the attention from both research and industry communities. Throughout the spring of 2019, a total of 158 systems were developed and submitted to the 4 tasks (altogether 9 tracks) of this evaluation by 30 registered teams. Generally speaking, the state-of-art deep neural frameworks and optimization techniques are applied and discussed in CCMT 2019. With the fully awareness of the advantage and limits of the existing technologies in the literature, it is reasonable to expect new methods and techniques appeared in the next year.

CCMT 2019 is still, to some extent, centered around the classical tasks in MT community (with the exception of the speech translation task, as well as the word level quality estimation track). With the fast-growing acceptance to MT technologies and systems, translation agencies are faced with new challenges. CCMT would like to bridge the gap between the MT research community and the translation industry community, inviting new tasks and tracks for the following evaluation campaigns.

Acknowledgments. Our special gratitude goes to partners who providing the data resources (with no special order): Alibaba (China) Co., Ltd., Baidu inc., Beijing Lingosail Tech Co., Ltd., DianTongShuJu Co., Ltd., Northeastern University, Harbin Institute of Technology, Nanjing University, Inner Mongolia University, Qinghai Normal University, Northwest Minzu University, Tibet University, Xiamen University, Institute of Intelligent Machines. CAS, Institute of Computing Technology (CAS), The Xinjiang Technical Institute of Physics & Chemistry (CAS), and Institute of Automation (CAS). We would also express gratitude to the Technical Committee of Machine Translation of CIPSC and all the participating teams for their various supports and contributions to CCMT 2019 evaluation campaign.

References

Huang, S., Jiaermuhamaiti, Y., Zhao, H., Liu, Q.: The 14th China workshop on machine translation (CWMT 2018) evaluation report. In: The 14th China Workshop on Machine Translation (CWMT 2018), Wuyishan, China, 25–26 October 2018

Wang, K., Jiang, W., Yang, H., Xiang, L., Zhao, H.: The 11th China workshop on machine translation (CWMT 2015) evaluation report. In: The 11th China Workshop on Machine Translation (CWMT 2015), Hefei, China, 24–25 September 2015

Zhao, H., Xie, J., Lv, Y., Yu, H., Zhang, H., Liu, Q.: The 9th China workshop on machine translation (CWMT 2013) evaluation report. In: The 9th China Workshop on Machine Translation (CWMT 2013), Kunming, China, 31 October–1 November 2013

Barrault, L., et al.: Findings of the 2019 conference on machine translation (WMT19). In: Proceedings of ACL 2019 Fourth Conference on Machine Translation (WMT19), Florence, August 2019

Vaswani, A., et al.: Attention is all you need. In: Proceedings of Advances in Neural Information Processing Systems, pp. 5998–6008 (2017)

Sennrich, R., Haddow, B., Birch, A.: Improving neural machine translation models with monolingual data. In: Proceedings of the 54th Annual Meeting of the Association for Computational Linguistics (Volume 1: Long Papers), pp. 86–96 (2016)

Ott, M., et al.: FAIRSEQ: a fast, extensible toolkit for sequence modeling. In: Proceedings of NAACL HLT 2019 (2019)

Author Index

Printed in the United States
By Bookmasters